Conquering Shame
and Codependency

Conquering Shame and Codependency

8 Steps to Freeing the True You

Darlene Lancer, J.D., L.M.F.T.

Hazelden Publishing

Hazelden Publishing
Center City, Minnesota 55012
hazelden.org/bookstore

LIBRARY OF CONGRESS CATALOGING-IN-PUBLICATION DATA
Lancer, Darlene.
    Conquering shame and codependency : 8 steps to freeing the true you /
    Darlene Lancer.
        pages   cm
    Includes bibliographical references.
    ISBN 978-1-61649-533-6 (paperback) — ISBN 978-1-61649-530-5 (e-book)
    1. Codependency.   2. Interpersonal relations—Psychological aspects.
3. Shame.   4. Self-esteem.   I. Title.
    RC569.5.C63.L36 2014
    616.86—dc23

                                                        2014008694

EDITOR'S NOTE
The names, details, and circumstances may have been changed to protect the
privacy of those mentioned in this publication.

This publication is not intended as a substitute for the advice of health care
professionals.

Alcoholics Anonymous and AA are registered trademarks of Alcoholics
Anonymous World Services, Inc.

The brief excerpts on pages 14–15 and 18 are from pp. 75, 76 from *How People
Change* by Allen Wheelis. Copyright (c) 1973 by Allen Wheelis. Reprinted by
permission of HarperCollins Publishers.

The quote on page 152 and table on page 16 are adapted from *Shame and Pride:
Affect, Sex, and the Birth of the Self* by Donald L. Nathanson. Copyright (c) 1992
by Donald L. Nathanson. Used by permission of W. W. Norton & Company, Inc.

18   16   3 4 5 6

Cover design: Theresa Jaeger Gedig
Interior design: Cathy Spengler
Typesetting: BookMobile Design and Digital Publisher Services

To the memory of Richard H. Brown and the futures of Jacob, Eliyah, Scarlett, Sloan, and Elisheva

Turnaround

When did you turn left
Instead of turning right?
A long, long time ago
You faded out of sight.

You danced a tune for others' eyes
And sang for others' ears,
Slowly donning each new guise,
Your own voice waning through the years.

Neglected needs and buried dreams
Secreted by shame,
Truth sacrificed for love,
Still failed to curb the pain.

Up and down the road again,
Attempting to reclaim,
Trying to remember when
You silently forgot your name.

Turn inward love, and listen,
Your own voice faint you'll hear.
The only one you've longed to love
Was always waiting near.

By Darlene Lancer 1998, 2014

Contents

Acknowledgments

I'm appreciative to Sid Farrar for asking me to write on this important topic, to Peter Schletty for his valuable and thoughtful assistance, and to the Hazelden staff in finalizing this book. It's with deep respect that I acknowledge the painstaking analyses and scholarly treatises of Karen Horney and Silvan Tomkins as well as the invaluable insights of Gershen Kaufman.

Introduction

In 1979, I started attending Al-Anon, a Twelve Step group for family and friends of alcoholics, to help an alcoholic in my life. I was offended when someone said that *I* had a problem. But beneath my veneer of superiority, in both my professional and my personal life, was a frightened, lost little girl. I was what therapists call "codependent," and, like many codependents, I didn't fully trust or value myself or even know who I really was outside of the roles I played. I'd given up so much of my real self in my primary relationship that I'd become isolated from my friends and family. I'd stopped trying new things and didn't take pleasure in activities by myself—I wouldn't even watch television alone! I'd lost touch with my feelings and stopped thinking about my needs. Instead, I readily accepted blame for my situation. Bit by bit, I was dying inside—so slowly that I didn't notice it.

Despite being unhappy, I was in love, and romance gave me hope that love would make the relationship work and bring me happiness. I was unaware of the cause of my problems and had a bad case of the "if onlys"—*if only he would change.* But he was addicted to alcohol. Instead of making changes myself, I reacted, daydreamed, and made excuses. Rather than value my needs and set limits, I believed broken promises, rationalized, and continued to accommodate the alcoholic. I worked harder and harder to make the relationship work and become who he wanted or needed me to be. I felt guilty if I didn't measure up to his expectations or how I imagined I *should* be. It never occurred to me to set boundaries or put my energy into developing myself. I was a textbook example of codependency.

It took time for me to trust Al-Anon, but eventually I understood that I was attending meetings for *me*. I got to know myself, improved my self-esteem, developed friendships, discovered new activities, and became more assertive. I found the courage to leave that relationship and my profession and to become a marriage and family therapist—a livelihood more suited to my true self.

Yet even after that relationship ended, my experiences with men continued to belie my conscious belief that my self-worth was now intact and that I deserved love. Although I wasn't being abused, I rationalized settling for less than I needed. I discovered that I lacked kindness toward myself and that I never really felt lovable, even as a child. I had found the enemy—and it was me. Shame, along with fears of rejection and abandonment, had ruled me. They caused me to be defensive and to hide, doubt, and judge myself, rather than honor what I truly wanted. Most damaging was that shame had caused me to make poor decisions that had traumatic consequences. In addition, a series of rejections, losses, and health problems revealed the depth of my shame and challenged my will to live. Despite all the gains I'd made, I had to dig deeper, examine my beliefs, and heal my shame and codependency from the inside out, one thought at a time.

Helping people uncover and recover their true self and proudly stand up for who they are, without apology, is what I'm most passionate about. It's work I've been doing personally and with clients for decades. I imagined the subtitle for this book to be "Love's Silent Killer" (the title of chapter 6) because I've learned that that is what shame is. Shame destroys our dreams and stifles our talents, and as much as we want to love and be loved, it sabotages our relationships. As I researched and wrote *Conquering Shame and Codependency*, the insidious way shame undermines us became even clearer to me. My work with individuals and couples became more focused and effective. My clients' self-awareness, moods, and behaviors exponentially improved. Healing shame is powerful medicine.

Shame and disconnection from our authentic self lie at the core of codependency and addiction. It's as if we've lost our true self, leaving an emptiness filled with anxiety and restlessness. By necessity, our focus becomes external—the main symptom of codependency. This relieves our pain, but doing so increases our self-alienation, which creates an ever-increasing need to look outside ourselves. This habit becomes a circular, self-perpetuating system that takes on a life of its own.

At times, our thinking becomes obsessive, and our actions become so compelling that they have a compulsive quality we can't control, despite adverse consequences. Twelve Step programs call it "self-will run riot." This is why codependency has been referred to as an addiction, even though it doesn't seem as obvious to us as someone unable to stop an addiction to a substance or an activity, like gambling or working. This is our denial—a major symptom of codependency and addiction. However, in this book, when I use the term *addict*, I'm referring to alcoholics, gamblers, and other addicts addicted to a substance or activity—but not precluding their codependency.

Other chief symptoms of codependency are dependency, a need to control, and personal boundary problems. Shame is interwoven throughout these symptoms and is the common denominator of others, like low self-esteem, painful emotions, high reactivity, perfectionism, intimacy problems, non-assertiveness, and caretaking. You may relate to some of these, but not to others, because codependency and shame exist on a continuum. Some codependents have full-blown symptoms that destroy their lives, while others have mild or occasional symptoms.

Denial is the biggest obstacle to healing, and the denial around shame is immense, undoubtedly because shame is our most painful emotion. Some people who have belonged to a Twelve Step program for decades are unaware of how deeply shame controls them. They may appear successful and function well, yet their worth is still dependent on others' validation. At the other extreme, shame can make us want to die or live a deadened, alienated existence. Shame isn't discussed much publicly, and it's the elephant in therapy rooms that is rarely addressed. People come to therapy to *change* who they are rather than *accept* who they are. But when we're not conscious of our shame, we're robbed of our power to take risks, to love and protect ourselves, and to realize our goals.

Conquering Shame and Codependency takes an in-depth look at shame as a primary cause of codependency and addiction. At first, some of this material may be difficult to fully absorb. Focus on the concepts that resonate with you. If you reread the book later, you may find it more meaningful. Each chapter builds organically on the preceding one, starting with an overview of shame and how it affects codependents in particular. There are case examples, which are predominantly drawn from composites of individuals. You'll learn what shame looks and feels like, understand the roots of your shame, and begin to recognize how it manifests in your life. If this is all you get out of the book, you will be miles ahead of most people when it comes to understanding themselves and others. You may be shocked, in fact, to discover how much shame impacts almost everyone. Although we don't heal our shame merely through intellectual knowledge, if you do the exercises outlined at the end of each chapter and in chapter 8, you will have more than knowledge— you will have the tools to connect with your real self and will start to see some incredibly positive changes in yourself. You will begin to heal, and your life and relationships will reflect this healing.

Although we have to be able to feel to heal, feeling pain when we're all alone can reinforce a familiar pattern of suffering in isolation. Shame first develops in early relationships and is healed in an atmosphere of acceptance and belonging. To fully recover, it's essential to do this work with a trusted and experienced sponsor, counselor, or psychotherapist. This is particularly true when we've experienced trauma, which most codependents have to varying degrees. But there is a lot you can do on your own to witness positive results.

Healing from shame and codependency is possible, and it is one of the most liberating things you will ever do. My sincere hope is that this book will illuminate and further your journey toward recovering and honoring the unique qualities of your true self.

The Shame Experience

There I was, on the floor in the hallway of my junior high school, in a shoving, hair-pulling scuffle with a gang member who'd been badgering and insulting me all week. Gawkers gathered around, including about a dozen boys from my class. Making a scene was embarrassing, especially because my skirt flew up. But later, when I discovered a small rip in my panties, I was mortified! Not only had my modesty been scarred, but my defectiveness, symbolized by the damaged panties, had been exposed. I dreaded returning to school. How could I face those boys? Luckily, no one mentioned the incident or my panties—and they most likely never saw the tear—but for days I imagined that everyone was mocking me.

That is the essence of shame. Shame can feel as if we were wearing dirty underwear *that everyone can see*. But shame doesn't stop there. Shameful feelings can linger, tormenting us for days and even years after we've been humiliated, rejected, or in a situation where we felt somehow defective.

The need to belong and feel accepted is one of the most basic and primal of all human needs, and it dates back to the beginning of time, when survival was a tribal effort. Belonging provides a sense of internal security. When that is interrupted, the magnitude of feeling different, inadequate, or inferior can be unbearable. When shame becomes chronic, it can take over our identity and our ability to enjoy life, chipping away at the trust we have in ourselves and the world. It's the feeling of being a bad or unworthy person. And it underlies all addictions.

As was the case in my junior high school incident, most of us associate shame with feeling exposed (in my case, literally and figuratively) in front of others. But an audience isn't always required. More often, shame is silent, secret, and self-inflicted, caused by our beliefs about ourselves. No one need be present to evoke the private angst of self-judgment. We *imagine* others see and judge us as we judge ourselves. When we measure our thoughts, feelings, and behaviors against the self we'd like others to see, we realize the full weight of the inadequacy.

We can choose to interpret any aspect of ourselves—our appearance, income, status, feelings, or behavior—as a reflection of our inadequacy. We might feel disgust about our body, so we decline invitations to the beach or a swim party. We might feel stupid for running out of gas, so we don't explain to our boss why we're late. We might feel like a failure for not achieving a goal, so we give up on our dream career. Or we might feel pathetic for grieving a divorce "too long" or undesirable when we're lonely, so we conceal our emotions rather than talk about them.

Shame is a heavy cross to bear day in and day out, yet none of us wants to be called *shameless*. That's because it's normal to have a certain level of shame. It encourages us to adhere to socially accepted norms, such as basic manners or how we present ourselves. On the other hand, too much shame, and shame about the "wrong" things, sabotages relationships and can lead to antisocial behavior, addiction, and codependency. It lurks in the unconscious, undermines self-esteem and confidence, and creates anxiety and havoc in our lives. In short, it can make us and everyone around us miserable.

Shame typically begins at an early age, and it also can be passed down generationally. Some parents teach their children to keep secrets to maintain appearances and to hide family shame about addiction, mental illness, criminality, infidelity, poverty, or a pregnancy out of wedlock. Sometimes children are shamed at home or at school for not measuring up in one way or another. The behaviors of family members (or those close to us) that violate our own standards can cause us to feel vicarious shame and humiliation. For example, a wife might be ashamed of her husband's rudeness in a restaurant. She then imagines that other patrons are judging them both—him for his rudeness and her for staying with him. Her husband's failure to measure up to her own ideals causes her to feel self-consciousness, self-judgment, and shame. Her belief that others are judging her is a defense against her own personal shame more than her husband's embarrassing conduct at one meal. If we were to ask her, "If you saw a couple in a restaurant and the husband was acting rude, would you judge his wife?" she'd probably reply that she wouldn't. In fact, most people would probably sympathize with her. Often, we think people are judging us or judging our loved ones when they're not.

Universal and Inevitable

Shame is something all of us feel. Although Americans aren't in the habit of discussing shame, the shame experience is pervasive in this country. We might never share our stories of shame, or only reveal them to a select group of people, but we all have them—and we tend to remember them as if they happened yesterday.

In other parts of the world, however—particularly in Asia and other societies that place a high value on honor, reputation, and community—people openly talk about shame. They even value it as a means to modify behavior. Mencius, a Chinese philosopher, wrote that "a sense of shame is the beginning of integrity." In China, it's viewed as "the ability or tendency to . . . take delight in the performance of one's duty," and in Japan, failure and negative self-evaluation are regarded as motivation for positive change.[1] In collectivist cultures—where the family, clan, or community is more important than the individual— one person's actions can shame an entire group. A woman who went to high school in Soviet Russia recounted her horror the morning she arrived at school to see a huge sign posted on the building. She'd gone on a date with an American student who was visiting the school. The sign publicly questioned her national loyalty.

Custom and religion can also influence shame. In some cultures, when a wrong can't be corrected, suicide is considered an option. For example, in Japan, suicide was historically the ultimate means of saving the family's honor. South Korea has a high incidence of suicide among students and the elderly. Students feel extreme pressure to perform well on college entrance exams, and if they do poorly, they see suicide as a viable option. It's not uncommon for elderly South Koreans to commit suicide out of a sense of sacrifice, to relieve their children of the growing burden of supporting them.[2] Mexico is an example of a Christian shame-based society, where preserving honor and appearances takes precedence over individual needs.[3]

In some cultures, divorce and loss of chastity are sources of shame. Until recently, in much of Africa, women without a clitorectomy were shamed and considered unmarriageable. In many Western societies where independence is highly valued, people who have trouble taking care of themselves may feel inadequate. They're often too embarrassed to seek help and feel ashamed or needy for wanting to be loved and held. In the West, we view shame as making us weak and inferior. The experience of shame itself feels shameful.

We can break the shame experience down even further by looking at men and women within a culture. Generally speaking, men value strength, emotional control, work, and virility. Any sign of weakness—such as crying, being unemployed, or being sexually inadequate—can elicit shame in many men. Women in cultures where sexual modesty is valued might feel shame about expressing their sexuality. In the United States, where beauty and thinness are prized, women can easily feel shame about a flaw in their appearance. Women experience more shame than men and tend to attack themselves, while men tend to attack others.[4]

Shame is inevitable—it is part of our human condition. From birth to death, our environment, relationships, and limitations challenge our identity and self-esteem. Unless we're fortified with the coping skills needed to be resilient in the face of shame, we can naturally feel a sense of failure and disappointment in not meeting our expectations and those of others.

Young children are particularly vulnerable because they depend on adults for security, love, and the fulfillment of so many needs. School performance and acceptance by their peers, and later their romantic interests, are critical for school-aged children and adolescents. Becoming independent and self-supporting is a milestone that, if not reached, can trigger a sense of failure for not meeting societal norms for success. Illness, disability, and aging can foster shame, as can loss of property, employment, relationships, or status. Public condemnation for unethical conduct is humiliating, but even minor occurrences can be catalysts for shame—talking too much or too little, for example, or simply being forgetful. Whatever we feel ashamed of, at its foundation is an often unconscious belief of inferiority or unacceptability—of being unlovable.

Subtle Distinctions

In the United States, we relate more to feelings of shyness, embarrassment, and guilt than to shame. In his scholarly treatise, psychologist Silvan Tomkins concludes that shyness, embarrassment, humiliation, and guilt all share the root affect of shame—a feeling of inferiority—although the meaning, experience, and intensity differ.[5]

Shyness

Shyness is the fear of strangers. A toddler might hide behind her mother's skirt when a stranger comes into the room, for example. Such behavior is considered normal early on, but later shy youth may feel pressure to be outgoing and more communicative. If they're unsuccessful, they may come to believe they're inadequate compared to their more extroverted siblings or classmates. Later in life, shyness can often take the form of painful self-consciousness with fears of being judged, rejected, or appearing stupid or foolish—even with close partners. Sometimes, even as adults, prolonged eye contact, dating, or kissing someone new can make us feel like timid teenagers. We may blush or feel tongue-tied. Underneath our shy behavior is a core fear of exposure and shame.

Embarrassment

Normal everyday interactions can trigger underlying feelings of inferiority as well. Although we don't usually identify this as shame, we will admit to feeling embarrassment. We might feel embarrassed over a social faux pas, such as forgetting a friend's birthday or addressing someone by the wrong name. The more self-conscious we feel, and the longer that feeling lasts, the more it actually feels like shame. What is mildly embarrassing to one person, such as having a credit card declined, may be painful to another. Compliments or positive attention can be as embarrassing as being publicly scolded. Too much attention can not only fluster us but may precipitate so much self-consciousness that we emotionally dissociate or numb our mind and emotions. When our reactions are this extreme, our embarrassment can be an expression of a deeper shame.

Humiliation

The word *humiliation* is often used interchangeably with shame, but humiliation focuses on the actions of another person, usually someone who assumes a position of power over us. When we're humiliated, we may or may not feel ashamed. Donald Klein writes, "People believe they deserve their shame; they do not believe they deserve their humiliation."[6] If we carry around enough shame, we may accept humiliation as if it were justified. The opposite is also true. Shame distorts perceptions, so we may feel humiliated by someone even when the person has done nothing to humiliate us. For instance, Joan, a client of mine, was distressed about a visible scar she had from an operation. When her sister Hilary casually mentioned that it could be surgically corrected, Joan became irate, insisting that Hilary had humiliated her by thinking her scar repulsive. It was Joan who found her disfigurement repulsive, and nothing Hilary said could sway Joan's interpretation. Reacting to humiliation with extreme anger is often an attempt to ward off underlying shame. The stronger the reaction, the deeper the shame. When I write about humiliation, I'm referring to when it also triggers shame, which needn't be consciously felt. For example, abuse generally causes feelings of both humiliation and shame.

Guilt

Many of us confuse guilt with shame. Guilt results from violating rules or moral precepts, while shame emanates from breaching accepted group norms. We're guilty if we *do* something bad. With shame, we believe that we ourselves *are* bad or inadequate in some way. Deep-seated shame can paralyze us and prevent us from taking action, even when we've actually done nothing wrong. In contrast, guilt can move us to address our behavior and take responsibility for our actions. In this way, as awful as it may feel, guilt can be a constructive emotion.

This "healthy" guilt is prompted more by a healthy conscience than by shame. It makes us focus on others, our effect on them, and on making amends. We feel the burden of guilt, and we look for a way to make things right so we can have a clear conscience. We know that we've done something wrong and want to fix it. We know, for instance, that lying is bad. If we lie to our spouse, we feel guilty. To repair the damage, we admit to lying and apologize. The purpose of guilt is to increase our empathy for others as well as repair our self-esteem. Taking action to relieve guilt feels good and constructive. We don't want to feel guilty again; we're encouraged to follow our moral compass and tell the truth in the future. In this way, by keeping us honest, guilt has done its job.[7]

Releasing guilty feelings by making amends comes more naturally for some of us than for others, but it is an ancient idea that has benefited society for years. Judaic law requires that one seek forgiveness at least three times from the person one has harmed. Making amends is the purpose of Step Nine in the

Twelve Steps of Alcoholics Anonymous and other Twelve Step programs. It suggests making direct amends to those we've harmed in order to lighten the weight of a lifetime of guilt-inducing actions, large and small. Working Step Nine can be an extremely liberating and uplifting experience for people in recovery.

When we cannot translate shame into guilt and take corrective action, it draws our focus inward to something we do not know how to change. We become concerned about how others evaluate us. We fear their rejection and feel defective and unworthy of our relationship with them. The differences in how we process guilt and shame are illustrated in Table 1.1 below.

Table 1.1. **Guilt versus Shame**

Guilt	Shame
Judge behavior	Judge core self
Specific evaluations	Global evaluations
Fear punishment	Fear abandonment
External focus	Internal focus
Promotes amends	Promotes hiding
Leads to empathy	Leads to egocentricity
Focus on effect on others	Focus on others' opinion of self
Leads to self-improvement	Leads to anger and aggression
Feels redeemable	Feels irredeemable
Can lead to empowerment	Leads to powerlessness
Reduces antisocial behavior	Leads to antisocial behavior
Moral judgments	Moral and nonmoral judgments
"Guiltless" is good	"Shameless" is bad
No psychological symptoms (when shame-free)	Causes low self-esteem, anxiety, depression, and post-traumatic stress disorder (PTSD)

As we noted above, the same action can evoke both shame and guilt. We might feel guilty for not contributing to the office fundraiser and at the same time feel ashamed that we're "cheap," "broke," or "selfish." Pathological and irrational guilt may actually be shame in disguise. Beating ourselves up over acts we feel guilty about can turn into shame because we might feel there's nothing we can *do* other than be who we are. We may feel doomed. Not surprisingly, research indicates that shame lacks the adaptive functions of guilt. In other words, it doesn't lead to making amends, learning from our actions, and improving our self-esteem. Instead, shame is linked to addiction, eating disorders, and other psychiatric disorders such as depression, anxiety, and PTSD. It can also lead to anger and aggression, psychological abuse, low self-esteem, and suicidal ideation.[8]

Types of Shame

Now that we know what shame and its close cousins look like, we can break down the definition of shame into different categories. Psychologist Robert Karen identifies four categories of shame: existential, situational, class, and narcissistic.[9]

Existential Shame

Existential shame occurs when we see the objective truth about ourselves or our situation, such as when an alcoholic faces the fact that he's indeed an alcoholic, or a mother realizes that her self-involvement has caused her to neglect her children. Such moments of self-awareness are powerful motivators for change—for example, adopting an addiction recovery plan that will not only prevent us from continuing the harmful behaviors but guide us in making choices that improve our self-esteem and sense of self-worth.

Situational Shame

Situational shame refers to a transient feeling we have when we violate an ethical principle, interpersonal boundary, or a cultural norm, such as urinating in public, cutting in a ticket line, dressing inappropriately, or talking on our cell phone in a movie theater. Feeling ashamed for such behavior is normal in that it helps us make the changes necessary to conform to the social conventions we consider important for acceptance and belonging. Situational shame can motivate us to take action and correct our mistakes.

Class Shame

Class shame relates to social power and pertains to things such as skin color, social class, ethnic background, and gender. It occurs in societies that have rigid caste stratifications or disparate classes. Class shame is pervasive in America, where success is often measured by wealth and status, and where class and related racial and cultural differences often breed envy and shame. The "American Dream" can reinforce shame because it raises expectations and hopes that may be unachievable, thereby causing the poor or otherwise disenfranchised to blame themselves and feel inferior.

Narcissistic Shame

When class shame moves from the group to the individual (for example, a woman whose skin is lighter than the rest of her family's), it begins to resemble narcissistic shame, the subject of this book. The word *narcissistic* comes from Greek mythology. Narcissus was a hunter famous for his beauty. When he saw his own reflection in a pool of water, he fell so in love with himself that he stared at his image until he died. Narcissistic shame is the opposite. When we look at ourselves, we may feel ashamed and inferior. Our self-image and pride are wounded. This type of shame has to do with our individual self-worth and how we feel and think about ourselves. Narcissistic shame isn't contingent on a class or situation. It's shame that lingers and never fully goes away. As Karen writes, "It's more than a bad memory. To 'have shame' in this sense means we are burdened with a festering negative self-portrait against which we are repeatedly trying to defend."[10] Narcissistic shame is a lie that exhausts us and keeps us from living life fully.

How We Carry Narcissistic Shame

We typically experience narcissistic shame in two ways: acutely and chronically. We react shamefully to something (acute shame) when our interest or enjoyment is interrupted. Tomkins points out that this shame response is seen in toddlers and believes its purpose is to motivate the removal of obstacles to our interest.[11] Codependents also live with shame as a constant (chronic, or internalized, shame). Those of us who have internalized our shame know what it means to have "shame anxiety."

Acute Shame

Acute shame is an unexpected "shame attack." We may be enjoying ourselves at a party when we trip on the carpet and not only blush but are sure people see us as socially inept, so we're self-absorbed and self-conscious for the rest of the evening. We may be out having a nice dinner when we spill our beverage and instead of apologizing and helping to clean it up, we yell at the waiter for putting the glass in the wrong place on the table. Just about anything can ignite an acute shame attack that unexpectedly overtakes us while we're enjoying ourselves or others.

When I was a teenager, one of my girlfriends would look around at other students whenever I spoke to her. Assuming she thought I was uninteresting and inferior compared to them, I felt bad about myself. When we're speaking to someone who shows a lack of attention, we could simply feel indifference, irritation, or contempt, but if we're especially interested or enjoying ourselves, as I was in this case because I wanted her friendship, we can feel shame. We assume they're not liking our company because they can see the inadequacies we're feeling about ourselves. Similarly, if a relationship ends or a conversation or correspondence unexpectedly stops, we might interpret that loss as rejection, which triggers shame.

Shame exists on a continuum that ranges from mild embarrassment to severe mortification—not caring to live. There are differences based on individual temperament, past experiences, and the triggering event. Acute shame has many symptoms, some of which are physiological and caused by our autonomic nervous system. We may blush, feel dizzy or nauseated, or perspire. We may become numb, unable to think, act, or talk. It can even lead to a loss of muscle tone, as when children visibly slump and hang their head. As adults, in an effort to hide a shameful reaction, we may laugh, stare, freeze our face, tighten our jaw, or show a look of contempt.[12] In front of others, we often feel like an outsider, transparent and exposed. It seems as though people could look right into our eyes—the "window to the soul"—and see our worst selves, so we avoid eye contact. The expression "losing face" refers to such situations where we feel disgrace and can't face other people. The impulse is to become invisible and hide, when we actually desire to be accepted. These conflicting desires create ambivalence, because we don't completely want to break the connection with the other person. We only want to hide our "flawed" self.

Acute shame can bring about profound feelings of deficiency, defeat, inferiority, unworthiness, and self-loathing. Our attention turns inward, as we isolate from our surroundings and withdraw into closed-off self-absorption. We feel alienated not only from others but also from the healthy parts of ourselves. In turn, this alienation from the world is replaced with painful emotions, self-deprecating thoughts, and inner anguish. Clinical psychologist Gershen Kaufman calls it "inner torment, a sickness of the soul. It is the most poignant experience of the self, by the self . . . Shame is a wound felt from the inside, dividing us both from ourselves and from one another."[13]

Acute shame is a common experience for people with a predisposition for addiction and codependency. We may use alcohol and other drugs or attachment to others to compensate for the pain and just to feel "normal" in the presence of shame. Drugs, alcohol, or focusing on another person help bury feelings of shame, effectively removing the obstacle to our ability to function and feel adequate.

Internalized Shame

Acute shame occurs and passes, just like any other emotion. Yet with enough shaming experiences, particularly in our early, formative years, we begin to internalize the accompanying internal voices, attitudes, and images[14] and form deep-seated beliefs of inadequacy that feel permanent and irreversible. Shame can take over a child's personality, emotions, and identity and continue throughout adulthood, or it may gradually increase and dominate over time.[15] Psychoanalyst Allen Wheelis poignantly describes the lasting effects from his father's cruel domination:

> *As we can record on tape the radio signal of a voice—*
> *record directly from receiver to tape without interme-*
> *diate translation into sound waves—so now I continue*

silently, inaudibly to receive and record that message from my father who, having even in heaven nothing better to do, continues to send: "You're a lazy, low-down, no-account scoundrel!"[16]

Chronic, or internalized, shame is a pervasive symptom of codependency and addiction. It's an open, unhealed wound that can seep into our soul and spread like a virus, creating negative ideas about ourselves that silently eat away at our confidence, effectiveness, and happiness, often without our awareness. At this point, not only is shame intensified, but it *no longer needs an external event or another person to trigger associated feelings and thoughts. The original shaming event(s) and beliefs needn't be recalled nor be conscious.* Once internalized, shame shadows us. We can evoke it all by ourselves, through self-criticism, self-imposed standards or goals, or comparing ourselves to others. We generalize our shortcomings and mistakes—they reveal more than a particular flaw. They're absolute proof of our inherent inadequacy or inferiority, and they're made worse by exposure to someone else. Internalized shame plays a major role in shaping our personality.

Table 1.2 describes typical beliefs associated with the shamed aspects of ourselves. Each of us may have different beliefs, but underneath is a feeling of not being good enough. Our beliefs are known to us to varying degrees and aren't subject to reason. In other words, we hold them as "truths," despite obvious, objective evidence to the contrary. For instance, there are beautiful women who think they're unattractive, successful people who feel like failures and discount their accomplishments, thin people who are convinced they're fat, and creative, brilliant individuals who insist that they're ordinary because they feel inferior to those they admire and to their own ideals.

Table 1.2. **Shamed Aspects of Self** [17]

Matters of personal size, strength, ability, skill	"I am weak, incompetent, stupid."
Dependence/independence	Sense of helplessness
Competition	"I am a loser."
Sense of self	"I am unique only to the extent that I am defective."
Personal attractiveness	"I am physically unappealing. Everyone notices my ugly nose (hair, legs, etc.), which makes me a target of ridicule and contempt."
Sexuality	"There is something wrong with me sexually."
Issues of seeing and being seen	The urge to escape from the eyes before which I have been exposed. The wish for a hole to open and swallow me.
Wishes and fears about closeness	The sense of not belonging anywhere, of disconnection from family, friends, and community; a feeling of being unlovable. The wish to be left alone forever.

To the extent that internalized shame takes over our personality, we fundamentally believe people don't like us and that we're intrinsically unworthy of love. We're forever evaluating ourselves, often making disparaging comparisons to others. We tend to interpret everything through that lens, easily feeling judged, rejected, and defensive. We may take advice as admonishment, disagreement as disapproval, questions as blame, and even neutral remarks as criticism. We might interpret offers of help as pity, reinforcing a negative self-judgment. We might disbelieve praise and construe it as manipulation, shaming, or the result of another's lack of knowledge or discernment. Because we expect criticism and rejection, we're pessimistic about how our efforts will be appraised. Even when we receive a positive or balanced review, one negative remark or suggestion for improvement can wipe out any positive feedback and feels condemning. We may also be sensitive to hearing criticism of others, as if we were the one being criticized. When shame is pervasive, the anguish of internalized shame endures without end. The desire to hide becomes constant, generating perpetual fear of being exposed and painful self-consciousness.

Shame Anxiety

Internalized shame can deprive us of our freedom by creating persistent, debilitating anxiety that shakes our core identity. Shakespeare rightly knew that "Present fears are less than horrible imaginings."[18] Unlike the fear of a known danger from which we can escape, anxiety is apprehension about a future threat. It's the worry of not being able to preserve our well-being. Because the future is unknown, the mind goes round and round, contemplating dreaded possibilities.

It's normal to have anxiety about doing something dangerous, performing in front of an audience, or taking an exam. Such anxiety can motivate us to prepare and study. Internalized shame, however, exaggerates normal anxiety to the point where we become anxious about experiencing shame. This *shame anxiety* makes us self-conscious and hypervigilant about being exposed to others' judgment, rejection, or derision. It pulls us inward, limiting and distorting our relationship with reality and with ourselves.

Unconsciously, we ultimately fear abandonment. Shame anxiety is often disproportionate to any existing danger or arises when there's no objective reason to be afraid. It can seem as if we're being stalked by a nameless, phantom threat. We don't know where the enemy is or what to do. In Alcoholics

Anonymous, recovering alcoholics talk about a sense of "impending doom." We might awake anxious for no apparent reason or feel restless and unable to relax and not know why. It might be that we're reacting to repressed shame from the past that's being projected into the present, and anxiety about re-experiencing shame is a symptom of this unconscious inner battle.[19]

This terror that shame anxiety summons can cause us to restrain our words and actions and continually doubt, judge, and deride ourselves. Wheelis, in the story above, attributed his shame anxiety to his father's denunciation of him, which drove him "out of human society into the wilderness alone, thereby to confirm ever more deeply the image of myself as unworthy to live with others, have nothing to say, deserving of no recognition."[20] Following his uncomfortable withdrawal at a social event, Wheelis discovered that his isolation gave him something:

> *A weird safety, an obscure shame. If a slave should find himself in the drawing room with the master he would feel as I felt a few moments ago; and when, abashed at being so out of place, he should escape to the slave quarters he would feel as I feel now.*[21]

Falling Down the Well

After we have internalized shame, any shaming event can become magnified. During an acute shame attack, the symptoms balloon in intensity and duration. They can spiral out of control, regardless of whether the triggering event is internal or external, tossing us down a deep, dark, and lonely well with no apparent way out. (See Figure 1.1.)

We might feel as if our entire self is at stake, which can further amplify our shame. Typically, we replay the event over and over in an attempt to undo and control it, but this doesn't

Figure 1.1

Falling Down the Well of Shame

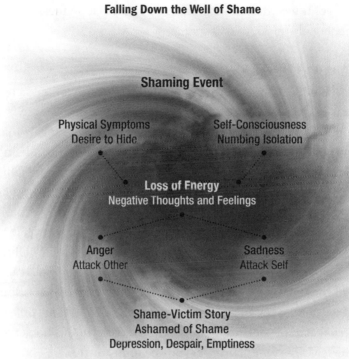

Shaming Event

Physical Symptoms   Self-Consciousness
Desire to Hide   Numbing Isolation

Loss of Energy
Negative Thoughts and Feelings

Anger   Sadness
Attack Other   Attack Self

Shame-Victim Story
Ashamed of Shame
Depression, Despair, Emptiness

help, and makes it worse. We find ourselves engulfed by negative feelings, such as rejection, fear, rage, sadness, worthlessness, loneliness, contempt, and self-loathing. Self-criticism escalates, and we may recall memories of incidents and feelings that reconfirm our personal story. In shame's painful grip, we withdraw and/or attack others or ourselves. This can last for months with temporary reprieves, or can be a constant burden. Though rare, at its worst, a single shame event can send some people sliding into a clinical depression. People who view their whole life through the lens of shame eventually may come to believe that they're nothing and have accomplished nothing. Over time, internalized shame can lead to loneliness, alienation, hopelessness, and despair.

Healing from Shame

There is hope. Now that we know what shame is, we can recognize it as it arises, and we can challenge it. Because shame is a common, universal emotion, conquering it doesn't mean that it's vanquished, but we do move from being a victim to being the victor. The objective is to manage and integrate our insights about shame into our personality, so that it no longer controls us or limits our choices. After a while, when we have a new experience of embarrassment or shame, we're able to acknowledge, examine, and respond to it in life-affirming ways that avoid "falling into the well." To our surprise, we discover that we're not reacting in the same old way. Shame becomes just another emotion.

I encourage you to buy a journal or notebook so that you can keep a record of your responses to the exercises in this book and of the feelings you uncover on your healing journey.

In the next section and in the following chapters, we will explore how we can break out of the shame cycle and come to understand how shame feeds codependency.

Exercises

1. Reflect on your shame-based thoughts and beliefs. You can add to the list. See if you can identify one of the following as your prominent core belief:
   - I'm unlovable.
   - I'm nothing.

- I'm a failure.
- I'm unwanted.
- I'm disgusting (or impure, dirty).
- I'm a bad person.
- I'm undeserving of happiness and deserving of punishment.
- I shouldn't have been born.
- I'm a fraud.
- I don't measure up.
- I'm flawed.

2. Think about the last time you had a shame attack and try to identify the underlying fears and beliefs that led to it. Do they match any you listed above?

3. When you have a shame attack, what happens to you physically (posture, muscle tone, eye contact, impulses)? What images come to mind? What emotions do you experience? Notice the pace, tone, and content of your thoughts.

4. The next time you have a shame attack, write about your experience in as much detail as possible.

5. What are things you can do to keep a shame attack in perspective and prevent it from overwhelming you?

Chapter 2

Shame and Identity

"The biggest disease today is not leprosy or tuberculosis, but rather the feeling of being unwanted." — Mother Teresa

Even if we grew up in a fairly healthy family environment, most of us can trace the roots of our shame to our childhood. Infants are born dependent and full of needs, especially the need for love and connection. Without it, their development can be severely impaired and they may die. In studies, well-fed institutionalized babies became ill, died, or developed psychological, mental, and behavioral problems, including lower IQs and mental illness, compared to babies raised by their mothers in prison or placed in foster homes.[1] The discomfort of hearing a baby's cries is meant to evoke a response in us. We're wired to want to ease their distress, care for them, and make them feel better. But it takes more than simply holding and even words of love to raise an emotionally healthy child. A child must feel uniquely wanted—that each parent desires a mutual relationship with him or her—and that his or her individuality is special, valued, and respected.[2] It's alarming how many children (including my own mother) have been told that they weren't wanted, that they were born despite an attempted abortion, or that they were the less-preferred gender. Those who are blamed for their mother's difficult delivery or a parent's problems can naturally infer that they're unwanted and unloved.

Love is first communicated to an infant through the mother's eyes, touch, and tone of voice. The way she holds, nurses, and touches her newborn conveys her own sense of security or anxiety, love or disinterest, attentiveness or impatience. She has to be able to adequately deal with her own exhaustion, anxiety, or frustration in order to be present for her baby's needs. Even in the first few weeks of life, an infant can sense displeasure and begin to withdraw.[3] Research shows that if the mother is expressionless while talking to her child, the baby begins to fret.[4]

As children grow, they adopt their parents' judgments, and this is observable in their play. Toddlers as young as eighteen months can show signs of self-consciousness and embarrassment. Between two and three years of age, they may show outward signs related to pride and failure. By three years old, they've sufficiently incorporated their parents' reactions, experiencing shame when they fail at a task, even when their parents aren't in the same room.[5]

How parents respond to their children's feelings and needs helps sow the seeds of either robust emotional health or codependency and shame. Codependency and shame co-emerge out of the same parenting. Each interaction between parent and child contributes to the child's ideas and beliefs about his or her identity. Depending on the frequency, duration, and intensity, parental reactions that are punitive, indifferent, shaming, painful, or fear-inducing can make a child—and, later, an adult—vulnerable to shame.[6]

The Developing Self

Most psychologists would argue that a distinctive core self resides within each of us that, under optimal conditions, manifests our innate potential. Just as an apple seed planted in nutrient-rich soil grows into a fruit-bearing tree, so it is with each of us. The type of fruit we bear depends on our intrinsic gifts, genetics, and temperament. Psychoanalyst Karen Horney identified that core self as the *real self*,[7] akin to the term *inner child* made popular by the addiction recovery movement.

If, as a child, we're allowed to be true to our real self, we express it in our adult life through our careers, hobbies, interests, personality, friendships, sense of humor, and a variety of other choices—whether deciding what to wear or whom to marry. Knowing our real self is important. It forms the foundation of our identity and keeps us true to our real purpose. The real self allows us to have full and meaningful lives and relationships.

But if our parents or parental figures deny, reject, or ignore parts or all of our real self, we adapt in ways that help us survive in our family environment by creating "unreal" identities. These manufactured identities camouflage and take us away from our real self, and they contribute to our misery in adulthood. In actuality, there are four non-true, divided identities (see Figure 2.1):

The Ideal Self (who we believe we *should* be)

The Persona (what we show to others)

The Critic (our inner shaming voice)

The Devalued Self (the result of the Critic's shaming)

Figure 2.1

The Developing Self

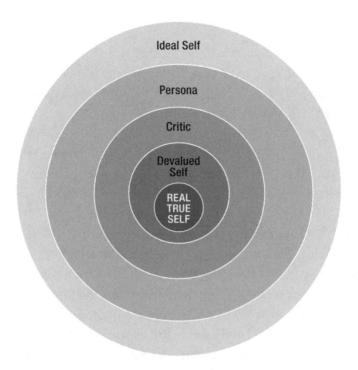

We'll discuss the Critic later in the chapter, after we learn some information about how childhood shame contributes to this identity. Here, we'll look at the ideal self and the codependent self, which often manifests in the persona and is a product of the Critic and devalued self—but not until we get a better understanding of what we mean by the "real self."

The Real, True Self

The real self drives us toward wholeness and expression of authentic feelings, desires, and innate abilities. With a healthy real, or true, self, we spontaneously respond to others by expressing what we feel—from joy to anger to sadness—and by communicating what we need and want without apology. Like the assertiveness of a toddler, our real self leads us to unabashedly say "yes" and "no," "I want" and "I don't want." Our real self makes decisions based on internal assessments without serious inner conflict between mind and body and thoughts and feelings. We feel "whole."

Our real self thrives in an atmosphere of warmth coming from people who allow us to express our thoughts, needs, and feelings and encourage us to fulfill our individuality. Our real self requires nurturing, authentic connection, and a safe environment, all of which give us a sense of belonging. Our parents' responses to our wants, needs, and behaviors are critical in allowing our real self to thrive. Healthy, affirming responses create a bond of trust that fosters our real self's development. To feel truly loved, we must believe we're accepted for who we are, not who our parents would prefer.

As children, we calculate how we want to be in the world through the many decisions that go into forming an identity. As we grow older, we create this identity by developing beliefs about who we are. We forge a true and healthy identity when our parents and others reflect our authentic, real self back to us, making us feel seen and heard.[8] Parents who put themselves in their child's shoes and try to understand situations from their child's point of view raise children who learn to identify and trust internal cues. When parents, for instance, accurately name and mirror their child's feelings and meet his or her needs, they affirm their child's true, or real, self. They empathize with and respect their child as an individual. These children then learn to own and trust their perceptions, thoughts, and feelings and gradually develop a whole, separate self through this matching process.

When a child lacks an empathic and understanding environment, painful isolation can result that causes anxiety and denies the child of the most basic of human needs—validation of his or her individual psychological existence. Children in these situations can feel "isolated and helpless" and develop "profound insecurity and vague apprehensiveness," which Horney refers to as *basic anxiety*.[9] Most codependents weren't loved as separate, independent individuals when they were young. Some of us suffered the "trauma of invisibility" and felt ashamed and empty in a confusing and uncertain world represented by our parents.[10] When children are not loved as separate, independent individuals, they can develop feelings of abandonment, helplessness, loneliness, and despair, as well as a longing to fill the emptiness. These feelings can also lead to anger that's often unsafe to express, especially as a child. Later in life, repressed hostility can manifest as envy, distrust, and contempt toward ourselves and others. These behaviors stand in the way of giving and receiving love.

The Ideal Self

When our parents don't foster confidence and expression of our real self, our authentic feelings gradually recede and become overshadowed by shame. Over time, as we internalize our shame, we reject the real self and construct a new identity by imagining a fictional self that is shaped by our personality, defenses, and experiences.[11] This ideal self serves to protect our real self and enable us to receive the love we need.

Our ideal self reflects how we think we *should be* in order to survive in the family, but instead of protecting our real self, the ideal self further alienates us from who we really are. For example, in a family where sadness isn't accepted, a child might envision being perpetually happy, even entertaining. This might mean being "the family hero," a "tough kid," or "a good girl." In contrast to a healthy ideal that reflects legitimate goals based on acceptance of the real self, including our shortcomings, our ideal self is a fixed idea that substitutes for genuine self-confidence and pride.[12] To the extent that we believe that this self-image is who we are, or should or could be, it can begin to seem more real than our underdeveloped and even disliked real self ever was.[13]

Our ideal self gives us an imagined sense of acceptance, worth, and superiority and provides an identity and path for self-fulfillment. It appears to be a wonderful solution because it alleviates the intolerable pain of internalized shame. Thus, perfecting the ideal self becomes compulsive. Rather than express our real self, we seek to express our idealized self, thereby changing the course of our whole life and development.[14] However, by striving to become this false ideal, we become even more alienated. We may choose a spouse, lifestyle, or career, as I did, all to win the approval of our parents or others. I took this detour by pursuing a career in law. I unconsciously thought that being a lawyer would gain my parents' respect, since they didn't support my original career goals—one of which was to become a therapist.

The Codependent Self

Codependency is yet another way to create a false "self" to compensate for shame—but it goes much farther than the creation of an ideal self. This false self is the persona that the world sees. The codependent is out of touch with the real self. Per my definition, a codependent is someone who can't function from his or her innate self, but organizes thinking and behavior around another person(s), process, or substance; whether addicted to a person, a process (such as gambling or sex), or a substance (such as food, drugs, or alcohol), they all share symptoms and characteristics.[15] The difference is the object(s) of a person's dependency. Codependency is a disease of *a lost self*,[16] depriving us of vitality, spontaneity, and self-fulfillment.

Each of us expresses symptoms of codependency to varying degrees. We may lack the capacity to decide, to will, to act, to want, and to determine the course of our life. This is self-alienation, which, along with insecurity and shame, weaves a common thread through our symptoms and behavior. Some of us have only a vague self-concept and don't know what's true or false about ourselves or others in our environment. We may feel confused and not know what we feel, what we believe, or what we stand for. Some of us may have strong opinions that are attached to our ideal self. The extent to which we can access our feelings varies and is limited by the strictures of our ideal self. For most of us, our emotions can lack spontaneity and depth, *except* in reaction to what someone else does or says. Alone, we feel empty or depressed, so we may be attracted to the enlivening effect of relationships filled with conflict and drama.

Like our real self and our ideal self, our codependent self is usually rooted in childhood, especially if one or both of our parents were codependent. Codependent parents with weak interpersonal boundaries generally see their child as an extension of themselves, rather than as a unique, separate human being. Even "loving" parents may do this. They're unable to empathize and instead use their child to support their self-esteem, fulfill their ideals, and meet their needs. Lacking the parental validation of the real self, the child must adapt to caregivers and circumstances to survive. The child begins to believe that his or her feelings and needs are wrong or unimportant. To obtain connection and approval, or at least safety, the child suppresses true feelings, needs, and wants. In the process, the child loses touch with innate cues and responses, which impairs the healthy growth of an autonomous self. As the real self recedes, codependency is born, impeding the child's natural individuation—the process of owning and trusting perceptions, thoughts, feelings, and memories and becoming a separate individual cognitively, emotionally, and psychologically. This is how codependency is transmitted through generations.

A persistent parental failure to empathize with and validate a child's real self, in addition to codependency, also generates shame. The parent's lack of emotional connection is felt as abandonment—a child's worst fear, as it means being unwanted. When a child doesn't feel understood or receive a responsive look in a mother's face, voice, and touch, he or she feels unlovable, alone, and doomed.[17] Children interpret emotional abandonment and disappointment to mean that they're bad, unimportant, inadequate, and essentially unworthy of a loving relationship. They blame themselves for being the cause of their parents' actions. When the break in the connection to a parent is only temporary or incidental, the love bond between a parent and child can be restored, especially if a parent recognizes what he or she did and apologizes. But when abandonment recurs on a regular basis, the child can lose the connection with his or her real self, which becomes shrouded in shame. (See Figure 2.1, where the Critic surrounds the real self.)

As codependents, we become invested in maintaining and promoting feelings and traits associated with our false ideal self, while hiding those that are inconsistent, in order to be acceptable to ourselves and others.[18] We suppress or completely repress contrary thoughts and feelings, which moves us farther and farther away from our true self. When we sense this inevitable gap between our ideal self and our real self, we can feel shame. And if we believe someone else senses this discrepancy, the shameful feeling can be excruciating. As shown in Figure 2.2, the devalued self grows in step with the gap between the real self and ideal self.

Figure 2.2

The Divided Self[19]

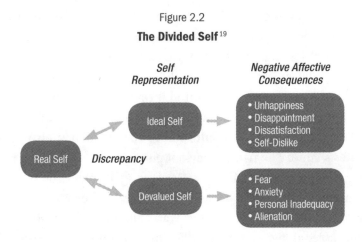

Self Representation   *Negative Affective Consequences*

Ideal Self
- Unhappiness
- Disappointment
- Dissatisfaction
- Self-Dislike

Real Self   *Discrepancy*

Devalued Self
- Fear
- Anxiety
- Personal Inadequacy
- Alienation

Parenting and Shame

Parenting isn't easy, and shaming isn't always intentional. The physical, emotional, and financial demands of providing for a family and sometimes extended family can drain parents' resources, leaving them exhausted, anxious, impatient, preoccupied, and depressed. Children of depressed mothers sometimes blame themselves for their mother's condition and lack of involvement.[20] Additionally, children have different temperaments and sensitivities, so a parent's behavior affects each child differently. Parents can shame their children by giving looks of disapproval, teasing, overcorrecting, withholding love, or showing indifference. As a result, these children often grow up to be shame-prone as adults. Ted, a client of mine, sadly told me about his parents' indifference when he received an invitation to join a prestigious orchestra. They had wanted him to focus on academics, not music. He felt invisible and misunderstood, as if he were an alien in his own family, and that nothing he did to express his real self would ever win their approval.

Even seemingly minor incidents have an impact. A child may interpret indifference, being ignored, or an irritable mood as hurtful and abandoning. I recall giving my father a soap carving when I was eight years old. "That's nice, dear," he said in a detached tone. I was crushed, believing he didn't like it. When I began to cry, he reassured me of his love with tears in his eyes. Had he not, I'd have felt unloved by him and believed that not only was the soap figure inadequate but that *I* was too.

Codependent Parents

Internalized shame can be passed from one generation to the next in how parents socialize and discipline their children. Yet, some codependents can't identify what was wrong with their childhood, because it seemed normal or even that they were fortunate. Even well-meaning, conscientious, codependent parents who are emotionally unavailable or lack a sense of self can inadvertently shame their children. They may subtly use them to meet their own emotional needs. Rather than heal their childhood wounds in therapy, these parents may try to reconcile with their children by parenting the opposite of how they were raised and unwittingly go too far. A parent who was neglected becomes over-involved, one who was controlled becomes too permissive, and one who was abused becomes overprotective. As a consequence, his or her children can develop codependent problems concerning autonomy, boundaries, and self-trust, respectively.

Unresolved Resentments

Many parents have unresolved resentments that seep into the comparisons they make with their children. A father may implicitly shame his son when he boasts about a skill or achievement or how hard he worked, suggesting that his son is inferior, ungrateful, or lazy. Similarly, a mother communicates envy when she begrudgingly compares her own paltry childhood wardrobe to her daughter's stylish attire. A childhood filled with such innuendos can cause considerable damage to a child.

Pressure to Try Harder

Some parents acknowledge their children's successes yet try to motivate them to do more or try harder. Pressuring children to achieve is often driven by a parent's own fear, shame, and feelings of inadequacy. Children may feel that whatever they do is not good enough. Barbara's parents repeatedly assured her that she'd have all she needed to succeed, and indeed they helped her with homework and paid for tutors. But when she didn't get straight As, she felt inadequate, like a failure, and ashamed of disappointing her parents. Because they provided everything she needed, she was convinced the problem was *her*.

Praise

Even positive statements, such as "you're a good kid" or "wonderful job," can be too general and cause a child to make general self-assessments and infer the opposite: "I'm bad (or terrible)."[21] If a parent offers no praise, too little praise, or too much praise, or alternates praise and criticism so that the child doesn't know where he or she stands, the child may become addicted to praise.[22] Susie, a talented singer, suffered from shame and low self-esteem because she received neither praise nor criticism growing up. She had no sense of herself or confidence in her ability. She was beset by self-consciousness and anxiety when she tried to relate to others.

Manipulation

Many codependents recall feeling unprotected, lonely, and misunderstood in their younger years. Some of us are perplexed because we were *told* that we were loved, but we were not treated with respect or love. Our parents may have believed that they loved us and were good parents; however, they may have lacked parenting skills or didn't know how to express their love. Some envious and hostile parents manipulate their children with love, opportunities, or material belongings, all the while reminding them of the sacrifices that they've made to provide these gifts.

Authoritarian Homes

In authoritarian homes, or those where addiction or abuse is present, children aren't respected. (When I refer to "abuse," I mean any type of abuse, including sexual, physical, and verbal, as well as emotional abuse, such as withholding affection.) Parents extract punishment and compliance through threats, withholding love, abuse, or humiliation. Shaming is often accompanied by anger or rage, and children walk on eggshells. They feel shame anxiety and eventually lose trust in their parents, other authority figures, and themselves.

When a parent's discipline system is based on "my way or the highway," children feel they have no choices or control over their life. Instead, the parent retains all the power. The message is that power is exercised "over" others, who consequently feel inferior and powerless. Children in these households can feel as though they have no rights, and that what they think and feel doesn't matter. A client named Nancy recounted how her father described her value in monetary terms by reminding her how much she cost him each year, adding that she had no "net worth."

In authoritarian families, as well as those with a drug-addicted parent, rules are often rigid, arbitrary, or inconsistent, and peace, praise, and punishment are unpredictable. Children's dignity and self-worth are undermined. They can feel power-lessness, rage, distrust, and inferiority, often vacillating between the extremes of being either rebellious or submissive. As rules keep changing, they try to please their parents, believing that if they do the right thing, they'll be accepted. Unfortunately, that's an illusion. They're continually made to feel they're wrong and not good enough, and they blame themselves.[23] Many of these children become overly self-reliant and seek independence and security in power, work, or money.

Blaming

A similar pattern appears in "blaming" families. When any-thing goes wrong, rather than focus on a solution, someone must be culpable. One shame-ridden spouse blames the other or blames a child. Family members are cast in the role of ac-cused or accuser. Pain and shame get passed down from an older or more powerful sibling to a younger or weaker one. This also happens in families where power is hierarchical. Each person finds someone weaker to boss around and humiliate. Sometimes a child may be tormented and traumatized by a sib-ling, and many parents don't realize how damaging this type of teasing can be. One child can end up the scapegoat who is teased or mocked by the entire family. These family roles and patterns often get replayed in adult relationships.

Parenting Styles That Reduce Shame

As parents, we're usually not all good or all bad. Most of us un-wittingly shame our child on occasion, but balance it out with healthy doses of love and encouragement.

Tomkins contrasts parenting styles that reduce shame with those that induce shame.[24] Whereas parents can induce shame by blaming, criticizing, punishing, and judging, parents can reduce shame when they excuse and forgive their children's mistakes and apologize for their own, are sympathetic to their children's failures, comfort them when they're suffering, and accept their children's shame, guilt, shyness, and discouragement without pressuring them to feel better or change.

It's not just how children are directly treated that counts. Some insensitive parents enjoy entertaining others with humiliating stories about their children in their presence. The way parents speak about and treat others in general is also influential. When parents judge, blame, talk about, or act toward others with contempt or disgust, including a class or group such as the "needy" or a minority, they're modeling this behavior to their children, who learn to treat themselves and others similarly.

On the other hand, if children are generally treated with respect and consistently comforted, supported, and guided to help themselves, they're better able to weather the disappointments and shame that are a part of life. They learn to trust their parents and develop the capacity for interdependence with fellow human beings. Children in these homes believe that others care and that help is available, and they're sympathetic and willing to help others.[25] They have the courage to accept pain, loss, rejection, and loneliness, and they have the tools to solve problems, all of which support individuation and identity formation.[26]

Shame Bonds

Just as a parasite attaches to its host, shame can bond with one or more of our feelings or needs. "Shame bonds" happen when, as children, we're shamed for needing help or being afraid or angry, for instance. The shaming doesn't need to be overt. A child can infer it from a parent's failure to respond to his or her feelings or needs. A mother who, as a child, wasn't held or whose distress wasn't comforted might intermittently or ambivalently comfort her distressed baby, or only do so with rocking or words and without touch or love. The baby could develop shame bonds related to distress and the need for touch or receiving comfort. These shame bonds can be insidious and very destructive. The degree to which shame-bound feelings and needs impact us as adults depends on how bound, or attached, our internalized shame is to these feelings or needs.

Once a feeling or need is shame-bound, we needn't have an external shaming experience in order to feel ashamed. *Experiencing the feeling or need itself triggers shame.* The shame bond can also disrupt our awareness of feelings and needs. We develop defenses to avoid experiencing the shame and the feeling or need. A man who feels ashamed of feeling vulnerable (whose vulnerability is shame-bound), for instance, might experience self-consciousness and shame in vulnerable situations, even if no one is being critical or shaming. He might even use a defense mechanism, such as denial or intellectualization (avoiding the unpleasant emotions by focusing on facts and reason) to avoid feeling ashamed or vulnerable. Codependents are commonly ashamed of and deny a great many of their emotional needs. Asking for needed help, comfort, or support would feel humiliating to them. Therefore many learn to become self-reliant, often taking care of others while ignoring their own needs, just as their parents once did. Some of the most common shame-bound feelings are distress, fear, and anger.

Distress

A woman whose feelings of pain or distress are shame-bound will have little or no self-compassion and disdainfully label

any thoughts about her pain as self-pity. Most likely, this woman's mother behaved as in the above example, or her parents
shamed her as a child when she would cry or complain. As an
adult, her shame makes coping with illness, pain, fatigue, loss,
loneliness, and problem-solving more difficult.[27] Having been
expected to solve problems alone, she grew up feeling isolated
and unable to trust others or ask for help. If her parents punished her for expressing her distress, she might experience fear
as well, making her loss and loneliness particularly frightening. To avoid feeling fear and shame, she will deny or ignore
her feelings. This woman will most likely avoid challenges
that might create distress and instead focus on, or even manufacture, external problems. She might lack empathy or even
have contempt for herself and others who are suffering and in
distress.[28]

Fear

Threats and reprimands for feeling afraid can create a fear-
shame bond. Boys in particular are frequently shamed for exhibiting fear. Their peers or parents may call them "sissies" or
"cowards" for not fighting school bullies, for example, or tell
them to "stop acting like your mother (or sister)." They may be
ridiculed and told to "grow up," threatened with, "I'll give you
something to cry about."

I was once asked to be a consulting psychotherapist for a
middle school ropes course. The challenge was to climb a thirty-
foot rope ladder up to a tiny platform, turn 180 degrees, and
then leap to catch a trapeze in flight. I did it myself and can attest
that the safety harness did little to quell my fear. One youngster
was very reluctant to even ascend the ladder; he'd climb a few
feet and stop. The counselor humiliated the boy each time he

pleaded to stop and descend. When I confronted the counselor, he felt justified that he was helping the boy gain confidence. In this example, the boy was shamed not only for exhibiting fear but also for showing vulnerability, distress, and weakness.

Laughing at a child's irrational fears is also shaming. As a child, I was repeatedly humiliated for feeling afraid. When I was little, my brother terrorized me by pretending to be a monster or claiming there was a big spider on my back. Everyone thought it was funny, which felt shaming. Another time, I told my mother that I was afraid to join a girlfriend who was climbing trees. Trying to cheer me up, my mother laughingly said, "Climbing trees is for the birds. One day your friend will want to be a lady, like you." Her remark, though well-intentioned, had an impact. After that, I repressed my shame and fears and emulated her, having only scorn for other fearful classmates.

Anger

Parents will also frequently shame their children for exhibiting anger. Often parents will do this as a means of control. Children are scolded for talking back or raising their voice: "How dare you raise your voice to me! Who do you think you are?" Girls are often told it's not "nice" or "ladylike" to express anger. Some people believe it's not spiritual or Christian to express anger. Parents often punish anger as a means of control. This instills a fear of retribution for anger and creates an anger-fear shame bond.

Growing up, I was scolded and sometimes punished for getting angry. For years, I repressed my anger. I might become angry at someone weeks after an incident or might not feel upset at all when I had every right to be. This led to passive-aggressive behavior—I would express my hostility indirectly, by procrastinating or being stubborn or acting out in some other fashion. One time, I heard myself saying the exact op-posite of what I felt. I said something loving, while deep down I was angry! (Technically this is referred to as a "reaction-formation" defense.)

In Al-Anon, my anger started coming out, and I needed to learn healthy ways of dealing with it. I stopped being passive-aggressive and learned to be assertive—to directly state how I felt about someone's actions—but it was a process. In the be-ginning, I felt guilty about being angry, especially at someone I loved. I discovered that this guilt prevented me from releas-ing my anger. I held on to resentment to justify my anger in my mind, but all the while I was becoming angrier. As with any emotion, once I accepted that it was okay to feel my anger, I could let go of it, along with my guilt and my resentment.

Positive Feelings

Even positive feelings can become shame-bound. Many par-ents, for example, don't allow their children to get "too excited" or "too happy," believing that it's bad luck or will create dis-appointment later. Parents who believe that pride is sinful may shame their children for feeling proud of an accomplishment. When these children become adults, they're rarely able to give themselves credit, confusing confidence with conceit.

Needs and Wants

Needs and wants, including drives for touch, appetite, and sex, are often shame-bound. Children naturally need and yearn to feel special and have a close relationship with their parents. Abandonment or rejection is shaming and makes them feel inferior or undeserving of love. One form of emotional aban-donment not previously discussed occurs when children have to "grow up" too soon by taking care of an ailing or addicted parent. Some parents neglect their children or are physically absent due to work, addiction, or other reasons. Parents aren't there for them, and they feel neglected. The message they may receive is that they aren't loved or important enough for their needs to be met, including their basic *need to have a parent*. Sometimes it becomes the child's responsibility to search for a parent in a bar, hide liquor bottles, prepare meals or drinks, care for younger siblings, call 911, or sober up a parent. Sometimes a child may have to listen to a parent's laments or diatribes.

Following a divorce, a child may be used as a companion to his lonely parent or take on adult responsibilities, becoming "mother's helper" or "the little man." These "parentified" children have to set aside their own feelings and needs to help their immature or needy parent. When these children become co-dependent adults, they often feel undeserving of love and resentful that they sacrificed their childhood.

Appearance and Behavior

Many things can be bound with shame. Children can be shamed about their body as well as such behaviors as a speech pattern, posture, or certain habits. Parents who focus on a child's appearance, criticize weight gain, and praise weight loss can cause their child to believe his or her appearance is all that the parents care about. It's easy for well-meaning parents to criticize bad habits, such as nail-biting, slouching, or hair fiddling. This rarely ends the problem and can make a child self-conscious and sensitive to shame on that issue. It's also shaming when parents disapprove in an accusatory tone or in a way that criticizes the child as a person, such as, "You look terrible," "The problem with you is . . . ," "That's disgusting," or "What's the matter with you?" If children have been socialized to work hard and be productive, and are judged for being lazy or passive, as adults they may feel ashamed and guilty when they become ill or unable to work. They may also feel unentitled to rest or to enjoy leisure and pleasure.

Shame bonds contribute to the general impact that shame has on us. The greater the shame bonds, the more shame dominates our identity and functioning. In terms of influence, the intensity of a shaming experience is inversely related to its frequency, so that one or a few intense experiences, such as incest, can be as damaging as years of ongoing, subtle, demeaning comments.[29]

We can't predict how being shamed in childhood will affect an individual later in life. Although parenting is a powerful influence, children have different temperaments, strengths, and limitations. Additionally, children are shaped by other adults such as relatives, counselors, coaches, teachers, religious leaders, and other adults in the community.

Moreover, how we cope with shame as an adult can either minimize or intensify its effect. Shame reactions and beliefs continue to develop in adulthood. Life events, illnesses, and careers can also boost or devastate our self-image. On occasion, a shame-dominated childhood doesn't significantly influence adulthood. Some people are able to harmoniously assimilate shame among their emotions. Others function well, until a shame-laden incident, such as a significant health, financial, or emotional loss, reignites childhood experiences of inadequacy and powerlessness, and they have fewer coping skills than those who have integrated shame.

A Divided Self: The Inner Critic

Shaming, abuse, and real or perceived unfairness breed anger in us as children.[30] However, when parents are manipulative,

indifferent, inconsistent, or interfering, children may not express this anger due to dependency on them and their love.
Expression of anger may also be disallowed or shame-bound.
Without a loving connection to our parents, we turn this hostility against our real self, which we've come to believe is unworthy
of love and respect. Our experience of shame is now intensified
and self-perpetuated by a shaming, devaluing voice, usually of
one of our parents, which takes up permanent residence in our
mind as an inner critic. It's as if a record needle were stuck, forever skipping and replaying the same critical inner dialogue,
often reminiscent of the parent's words. This voice continually
attempts to turn us into our ideal self in a tone that ranges from
mild frustration to one of malicious self-contempt. Whatever
the tone, we live with a punitive, persecutory detractor in the
background. This Critic, or inner judge, puts us in unending
conflict with our real self, as the drama of our childhood un-
folds internally.

In extreme cases, the Critic can overtake our personality to
the point that we feel nothing good or worthwhile about ourselves. We're constantly disappointed in ourselves and see only
flaws and failures. We no longer have access to our strengths
or abilities and believe every one of the Critic's accusations as
truth, and no one can convince us otherwise. The Critic compares us to others to reinforce evidence of our defectiveness.

Life with a harsh Critic can be paralyzing. The Critic can
find fault with any thought, feeling, choice, or decision. Our
self becomes divided into the judge and the judged, seemingly
with no escape, and we're bound to the scrutiny of an unforgiv-
ing inner master. A robust Critic is unyielding and dogmatic,
second-guessing everything. Codependents and perfectionists
become afraid of making a "mistake" because the Critic is with-

out tolerance or mercy, regardless of justification or relative considerations. It's easy for us to lose self-trust to the point that decisions and spontaneous action are impossible. Although we may be successful in our job or other roles, underneath festers the shame and anxiety that the Critic creates, forcing us to function from a weakened, divided self, without access to the real self for strength.

From childhood onward, the Critic expects the unattainable by insisting that we suppress authentic feelings and traits that conflict with our internal ideal. We conform to who it thinks we *should* be and what it believes we *should* feel, think, do, and need. This is true whether our ideal is someone strong and more powerful or someone self-sacrificing and cooperative. We suppress genuine feelings, such as fear or hurt in the former instance, and boldness or anger in the latter, to the degree required to measure up to our ideal. As a result, as codependents we strive to think, feel, and act the way we believe is "correct." When our actions don't match our expectations, or when our limitations prevent us from achieving our ideals, we're filled with shame. In actuality, we're expecting the impossible—to become someone other than ourselves.

Ordinary shame isn't projected onto others. However, as a defense to internalized shame, the Critic is judgmental and contemptuous toward others and also gets projected onto others if we imagine that we're being judged when we're not. Internalized shame sensitizes us to habitually feeling humiliated, rejected, and ashamed. Circular reinforcement of self-criticism and projection produces repeated self-fulfilling prophecies.[31] (See Figure 2.3.)

Figure 2.3

Cycle of Shame

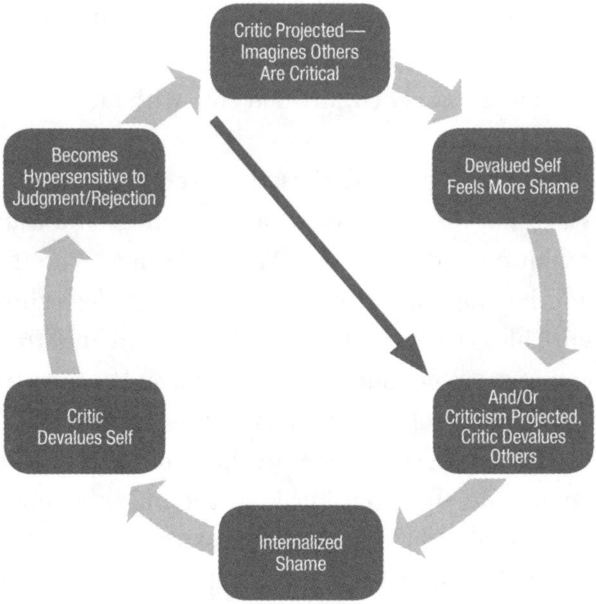

One reaction we may have to the Critic is to fight by disagreeing with it. Another is to disempower it and rebel against it like a teenager rebels against a strict parent. But these strategies don't help us. Instead, they can fuel self-hatred and damage our relationships. The consequences are also self-destructive. Many of us turn to drugs, alcohol, gambling, or codependent relationships to temporarily silence the enemy within, but our addiction only provides more ammunition for self-chastising and self-loathing.

An unrelenting Critic hinders the healthy self-examination we require for growth. In recovery, we need to take responsibility for our feelings and actions, and to the Critic this can feel like blame. Instead of gaining information in order to learn and change, the Critic triggers feelings of shame and the consequent defenses and reactions to it. Our self-judgment may be so overwhelming that we can't possibly assume responsibility for errors. I caution people in Twelve Step programs who are working Step Four that taking a personal inventory of their shortcomings can provide a feast for the Critic. Shame and self-criticism are rarely on the list. And even if they were, they would afford the Critic further evidence of inadequacy! If you're working through the Twelve Steps, talk about these concerns with your sponsor and ask him or her to help you identify where your inner Critic is getting in the way.

Exercises

To deepen your understanding about what you've read in this chapter, write about the following in your journal or notebook:

1. Did you feel valued, loved, and respected by both parents and your siblings? Write what you felt from and about each family member.

2. Was it safe to express your authentic or true self? Specifically, what did you hide? Recall your feelings about this.

3. How did your parents respond to your mistakes, failures, disappointments, and shame?

4. List your expectations regarding your ideal self—all the traits, values, skills, and behaviors you strive for. This

isn't meant to include fantasies, such as being a billion-aire or Hollywood celebrity, unless these are real goals that you expect of yourself. Can you accept who you are today, "as is"?

5. What and who influenced you to strive toward this ideal?

6. Write about life events and people other than your parents that influenced your self-image and sense of self-worth. Be sure to write about your feelings and any beliefs you formed.

7. What feelings did you have that were shamed? What did you experience when you expressed feelings? What were you taught and what did you observe? Do you judge any feelings today?

8. What did you experience growing up when you expressed your needs, such as needs for love, touch, play, privacy, autonomy, or being listened to, respected, supported, encouraged, valued, and appreciated? What were you taught and what did you observe? How do you feel today about asking for your needs to be met?

These exercises will help you develop empathy for the child you were who embodies your real self. Continue with steps 1 and 7 discussed in chapter 8 to further accept yourself and overcome shame.

Chapter 3

Escaping Shame

As you now know, shame is an incredibly powerful emotion. It can convince us we're bad or seriously flawed and that we can't do anything to change who we are. To avoid feeling bad all the time, we try to escape shame. As children, we adopt different strategies, determined by our disposition and our home environment, to survive in a world of powerful adults and to escape recurring feelings of shame and isolation. As codependent adults, we use these same coping mechanisms to feel loved and avoid the painful thoughts and feelings associated with shame that threaten our identity.

These coping mechanisms are our defenses against shame. Many of us strive to perfect ourselves in order to feel acceptable and seek validation by becoming pleasers. Others among us may despise weakness and behave aggressively, deciding that a strong offense is the best defense. Some of us withdraw to avoid conflict and the possibility of shame, become arrogant, or maintain a pretense of feeling happy to hide our shame from ourselves. We might distract ourselves with activities or addictions. Most of us use more than one defense to avoid experiencing shame. Regardless of how we cope, as codependents, we're all plagued by feelings of inadequacy and self-doubt and share some degree of self-hatred, even if unconsciously.

Common Defenses against Shame

Defenses[1] may be necessary when we're growing up, but they're not effective in the long run. A child with no power in the family might withdraw to feel safer, but it's dysfunctional to withdraw from adult relationships due to unfounded shame anxiety. Once we become adults, our defensive strategies tend to create more harm than they prevent. For codependents suffering from internalized shame, these strategies can be problematic when they become rigid and operate outside of our conscious control. Let's take a look at some of the most common defenses we deploy against shame. Some of the symptoms of codependency discussed in chapter 5, such as perfectionism, can also be considered defenses.

Denial and Repression

Many years ago, at a time when I thought I had good self-esteem, I had a dream. I was sharing a bed with a woman named "Shame," whom I didn't know, and whom I didn't want to know. The dream revealed to me that I was unaware of my shame, which had contributed to my codependency and would continue to create problems until I got to know "her."

Denial is refusing to believe a truth. We can deny that we're addicted to alcohol, for instance, even if we're dependent on it. We usually deny something because accepting the truth is too painful. Some people act shamelessly, as if they don't care what others think. Often it's not that they lack shame but that they're denying their shame and behaving as if it didn't exist. To them it doesn't—but others certainly feel their shame.

Repression is burying in our unconscious what we believe are unacceptable desires or experiences. If these desires or memories were to surface to our consciousness, we would feel too much anxiety. It's not uncommon for people who were sexually abused to repress memories of the abuse. As codependents, we sometimes suppress, or consciously turn off, thoughts, feelings, and needs, but denial and repression are our tried-and-true coping mechanisms. Yet, whatever we deny, repress, or suppress doesn't just go away. Instead, unbeknownst to us, it influences our behaviors.

We all use denial at different times to cope with something frightening, painful, or overwhelming. If we thought about our own death every day, for example, we would find it very hard to function. Denying an illness or medical issue, however, may prevent us from getting appropriate treatment. Similarly, lack of self-awareness about our shame can be a major obstacle to healing. Because it's so painful to feel unworthy of love and connection, most of us deny our shame, particularly if it's been internalized.

Many codependents admit they were shamed as children but minimize how it affected them or deny it altogether. No one comforted them when they felt shame as a child, so it wasn't acknowledged, accepted, and integrated. In effect, shame itself became shame-bound—their shame about shame kept them a prisoner to it. Some can recall stories of abuse yet deny experiencing shame as a child. These people have *internalized and repressed* their shame.

When shame is denied and not integrated, it can be easily triggered, making us vulnerable to spiraling down the well of

shame. For example, we might feel self-conscious about sharing an opinion at a professional meeting, not consciously aware
of our belief that we're unequal to our peers. We might be hypersensitive to a trivial criticism, not realizing that the innocent
comment exposed our belief that we're defective. Or we may
need constant reassurance or be easily rebuffed when our ad-
vances toward someone we're romantically interested in aren't
reciprocated, unaware of our doubts about our lovability.

Paradoxically, some of us do the very thing that brings out
our denied shame. To this end, an addict's feelings of powerlessness over an addiction might lead him or her to increase addictive and self-destructive behavior, thereby magnifying feelings
of humiliation. For example, Charles was struggling with sobriety. He went on a weekend binge, anticipating that his subse-
quent self-loathing on Monday morning would motivate him
to quit. Darla repeatedly phoned the man she was dating despite his objections. The rejection she received validated her
preexisting feelings of abandonment, unworthiness, and anger
at men. Ryan, an unruly student, purposely wouldn't study in
order to confirm his belief that he is a failure. Jonathan was
unfaithful, but left discoverable evidence of his affair in order
to get caught and be punished for his guilt and shame. These
individuals escalated their dysfunctional behavior in order to
feel their denied emotions. This is often referred to as a defense
called "acting out," where we act out our feelings in lieu of feeling them. Our behavior magnifies our shame so that it becomes
conscious and provides us an opportunity to face and heal it.

Withdrawal
Withdrawal is a part of the actual experience of shame. It's also
a defense motivated by the desire to avoid feeling exposed, which
could create even more shame. Withdrawal is usually a response

to shame anxiety, which makes emotional connection frightening, regardless of how much we desire it. While withdrawing from opportunities to connect with others may protect us from being exposed, it also denies us the opportunity to get close to others—something we long for. Researcher Linda M. Hartling writes, "because of the terror that often accompanies the yearning, we retreat into self-absorbed disconnection."[2]

Introverts are more likely to use withdrawal as a defense to cope with shame because their temperament predisposes them to naturally turn inward when under stress.[3] Many codependents withdraw after a breakup because they interpret the ending as a failure or rejection. It affects their self-esteem due to their underlying feelings of shame. As a result, they may give up dating altogether to avoid the shame and painful feelings of abandonment they experienced in the rejection.

An entire personality can be based on withdrawal to avoid shame by repeating lonely patterns established in childhood. Some children have such shame anxiety and lack of emotional safety that they develop an inner fantasy world—an alternate reality in which to live. Others might retreat into schoolwork, drugs, reading, computer games, listening to music, or watching television to avoid family tension and painful interactions. These types of defenses are different from relaxing, meditating, or daydreaming because they're detrimental to relationships and are usually a reaction to the Critic's voice finding fault with the self and others. The Critic projects self-hatred onto others, whom they avoid, considering them just as dangerous, judgmental, or rejecting as their parents were.[4] These individuals value self-sufficiency, create rigid boundaries, and avoid emotional connection because it might trigger guilt, fear, and shame.

Withdrawal doesn't stop our feelings of unworthiness, and

we risk being lonely at the cost of comfort and support of close, interdependent relationships.

Aggression

As codependents, we may use aggression, or forceful behavior, to cope with shameful feelings. Aggression takes many forms, including anger, rage, vindictiveness, blaming, fault-finding, and other types of emotional abuse. It also includes physical violence directed at others or their property. Aggressiveness is intensified if our perception of another's judgment resonates with our own self-judgment. In this case, we may react with rage. In other words, our shame is commensurate with the degree of our aggression. Shakespeare's famous phrase "The lady doth protest too much" is apropos here. Men are more prone to aggression than women, who are socialized to withhold some forms of it, such as violence. Still, women may express it indirectly through innuendos, passive-aggressive behavior, or even a look. Aggression can also be turned inward against ourselves.

Anger and rage are considered secondary feelings to shame. Anger pushes people away in order to create safety. It provides us with temporary relief from feelings of shame, which are usually unconscious, by transferring them to someone else. Anger is a reaction to our needs or wants being unfulfilled. When it escalates to rage, we're reacting to a perceived assault on our wounded self.[5] Rage may signal that someone has triggered an old injury, such as childhood abuse, within us. In some cases, we might simply be mimicking what we learned from an abusive parent.

We might also react in a vindictively aggressive way, retaliating against our offender in an attempt to reverse our humiliation and restore our pride. If our need for revenge is thwarted or not acted on, we're left with a sense of weakness that can exacerbate our original shame and anger over the injustice. For example, rape victims, workers demeaned by an intimidating boss, or children humiliated by a parent or stronger sibling or peer may feel powerless to retaliate and ashamed of not defending themselves. It's not uncommon for people to recall childhood memories of being bullied at school or teased by a sibling and confess that their greater shame is that they didn't stand up to their aggressor.

Blame aggressively shifts shame onto someone else. Blaming others is a typical defensive pattern that codependents use, not only when something goes terribly wrong but for everyday misunderstandings, failure to be accountable for behavior, fear of anticipated problems, or just about anything the Critic chooses to judge. Blaming can happen so automatically that the blamer is only mildly aware of it or never acknowledges feeling guilty or ashamed. Making someone else the problem allows us to feel better about ourselves, while having the effect of making the other person feel the way we *really* feel inside. Codependents already have low self-esteem, making it hard for them to admit to any mistakes. As mentioned earlier, accepting responsibility for our feelings and actions is fodder for our inner Critic. Instead of suffering self-judgment, we might blame someone else to avoid feeling guilt and shame and to support our own innocence.

Regrettably, I did this to my own children. Sometimes, when I was unable to keep a promise to take them to the movies, I'd blame them for not first cleaning their room in time. This type of behavior is common. Couples frequently do this as well. For example, Gloria complained in counseling about her anxious husband Jack, saying he always blamed her when they arrived even slightly late to a social event. In each case, the host was gracious and welcoming, and there were no repercussions—only Jack's embarrassment and shame for not meeting his internal standards of punctuality. As a defense, blame not only damages relationships but also harms the blamer, who continues to experience life as a victim of other people and circumstances.

Belittling, fault-finding, name-calling, and other forms of emotional abuse also shift personal shame onto others. Abuse is about exercising power over others to dominate them. It stems from feelings of powerlessness, inadequacy, and shame. Feeling superior and dominating others compensate for feelings of inferiority and are motivated by self-protection. The abuser may be reenacting abuse he or she received as a child. Sometimes a person is domineering in one setting and subservient in another. For example, it's not unusual for a powerful entrepreneur or corporate executive to be aggressive in business but unable to say no in intimate relationships.

Aggressiveness can also become a personality style, with hostile bullying, shaming, abuse, and defensiveness employed as typical reactions whenever aggressors feel hurt or afraid. Aggressive behavior damages not only relationships but also the self-esteem of the aggressor and the victims.[6] It inevitably creates more shame and undermines trust. When aggression is turned inward, it's equally destructive. Because this defense pushes others away, it can lead to loneliness, depression, and isolation.

Projection

Projection is another unconscious defensive technique. When we project, we disown and mentally or verbally attribute our unacceptable feelings, thoughts, or qualities to someone else. Because of our internalized shame, as codependents, we're commonly hard on ourselves, and we often project our self-judgments onto others. Projection is a coping mechanism because it helps us keep those unwanted feelings and qualities out of our conscious awareness. When our judgment is expressed, it can make the other person feel inferior, which is the way we feel inside. Even if it isn't verbalized, projection of judgment serves the same function: it protects our internal self-image and wards off shame. When we blame, we project our own responsibility, self-judgment, and shame onto someone else.

We can also project our own thoughts onto someone else, particularly self-critical thoughts or judgments of our inner Critic, imagining that we're being criticized. People who are insecure and repeatedly request declarations of love are projecting onto their partner their own belief that they're unlovable. In the earlier example, Jack also projected his Critic onto the host when he and Gloria were late to the party by assuming that the host would judge him.

We frequently project shame-bound feelings and needs onto others because these emotions are too objectionable to be acknowledged or expressed. We may see someone else as being needy and may offer help, while ignoring or being unaware of our own needs and troubles. We may project our disowned vulnerability onto the animals we comfort, yet we're unable to comfort ourselves. If we deny our anger, we might project it and worry someone is angry at us or wants to cause us harm. We may become paranoid, projecting our aggression onto others. We might also project feelings from prior relationships onto current partners. For example, Cathy was frustrated that her new boyfriend wasn't calling more often. She constantly worried that he was angry at her. When they talked, he dispelled her fears and anger, and she realized she'd projected her feelings toward her unavailable father onto her boyfriend.

We might also project positive traits and feelings as a defense. People sometimes project their love onto someone they're dating and insist that their affection is being reciprocated despite evidence to the contrary. This is an example of combining denial and projection to avoid the shame and painful reality of rejection.

Arrogance and Contempt

Sometimes we may use arrogance as a defense, become self-inflated, and feel superior to others in order to avoid our unconscious feelings of inferiority. Arrogance also shifts shame and involves a projection that others are inferior. Contempt, on the other hand, is hostile condescension—"looking down our nose" at someone. Contempt includes arrogance and also anger and disgust associated with shame. It becomes projection when we contemptuously see someone else as disgusting or inferior, characteristics we have disowned and feel disgust and shame about. Contempt underlies various forms of emotional abuse. Whether or not it's expressed, it compensates for our feelings of inferiority by making someone else feel small and inadequate. Although arrogant people may also be contemptuous, arrogance reflects their attitude about themselves, whereas contempt is their attitude toward others.

There are other ways that arrogance is distinguishable from contempt. With arrogance we feel embarrassed or ashamed and still want to connect with the other person, but when we add contempt, we want to cut ourselves off from those we disdain. Contempt might enable us to end a relationship, while at the same time providing distance from the unacceptable qualities we feel in ourselves.

Contempt may be learned from a parent who is dismissive or rejecting. Parents model their contempt in how they discuss others ("He's a good-for-nothing") and by name-calling and making dismissive remarks such as "You'll never succeed" or "What do you know?" Some parents compete with their children or derisively boast and compare their children negatively, saying, "When I was your age . . ." They might compare their children to each other ("Why can't you be smart like your brother?") or to kids in the neighborhood ("You never see Cindy next door leaving the house looking like that.")

For a narcissist, arrogance and contempt are a personality style to compensate for and ward off underlying feelings of shame. Narcissists try to make others feel their shame, which usually remains unconscious until they suffer a major defeat or loss of confidence.

Humor

Contempt can be expressed using humor as a weapon to sarcastically or mockingly put down others. This is a form of aggression. Unlike sarcasm, which hides shame, humor in the form of wit or even self-deprecation can be used to express and expose embarrassing or shameful things. It is considered a mature defense, because it's more conscious, is adaptive, and has fewer negative consequences. Instead of being laughed at, the humorist takes control by making people laugh and winning their regard. This soothes underlying feelings of inadequacy. It discharges discomfort while enhancing self-esteem, relationships, and pleasure, and it increases a sense of confidence and success. Television personalities, for instance, might joke about their mistakes to smooth over awkward, embarrassing moments. Someone more ashamed (or not capable of using such a mature defense) might seek to hide and feel paralyzed, rather than bring more attention to their shame with humor.

Humor used to conceal shame can become a personality style. As children, some of us learn to be entertaining in order to win parental approval and diffuse anxiety and conflict in the family. We learn to hide behind our false personality and don't allow anyone to see who we really are. An example is a class clown, who is ashamed and actually deeply sad and depressed. Using humor this way—constantly being "on" and living a lie—can be draining. My client John survived the terror of his violent childhood by using humor to ensure his popularity at school. He continued to use this defense as an adult to deal with his perfectionist wife and boss. Although it provided temporary relief, his humor distanced him from his own rage, shame, and despair and didn't help his relationships in the long run. By integrating these feelings into his personality, his self-respect grew and he established boundaries that improved his relationships and sense of well-being.

Envy

We exhibit envy when we compare ourselves with others or want what someone else has—a possession, accomplishment, or quality. Underneath this envy are feelings of shame and inadequacy. Although envy is an unpleasant feeling, it's better than feeling deprived and not good enough. Some of us regularly compare ourselves to others—for better or worse. Envy differs from admiration. Admiration reflects positive feelings about what we admire, but envy is a negative feeling. Envious people begrudge others, not liking the fact that someone else has what they don't have. Envious narcissists, in particular, tend to belittle, sabotage, or one-up others. They might even try to steal their ideas or relationships. To defend against envious and inferior feelings, narcissists sometimes project their own negative qualities onto the envied person and believe that they're being envied.

Self-Pity: The Victim Role

Sometimes we're not responsible for bad things that happen to us, and we truly are victims. But feeling victimized can also be used as a defense against self-hatred, shame, and guilt. The amount of victimization we feel is usually proportionate to the amount of unworthiness we feel. It may seem strange to think of this attitude as a defense, but, similar to blame, self-pity externalizes the cause of our bad feelings about ourselves. The victim thinks "poor me" and hence is blameless, even superior. Someone else might feel angry or sad about painful occurrences and then either accept them or seek solutions. But not the self-pitying victim.

Many codependents are victims of abuse. As children, they were helpless to prevent it. Often, abused adults feel they're powerless to stop abuse because of their circumstances or their low self-esteem. Some adult victims might provoke abuse to receive the punishment they believe they deserve, so they can then feel justifiable self-pity and anger toward "the abuser"; anger that originally was self-directed can now have an outlet for open expression.[7] Abusers use this defense, too. They feel victimized and justified in acting aggressively and then blame their victim.

A variation of the victim role is someone who refuses to discuss a conflict by claiming, "You're right. It's all (always) my fault" or "I already feel worse than you about it." This cuts off communication and denies the aggrieved person a chance to be heard and understood. Outwardly, it appears as if "the victim" is accepting responsibility, but in reality this is a defense. In essence, he or she is saying, "I'm already too wounded to hear you," so as not to have to hear about the hurt the other person feels, which would only add to the victim's guilt and self-hatred.

Avoidance

Another way we avoid awareness of our shame is through addiction, which anesthetizes painful feelings. As addicts, we try to escape ourselves, which is an impossible task. We use our addiction to manage our shame, whether it's an addiction to a person, a substance (such as alcohol, drugs, or food), or an activity (including shopping, sex, or gambling). We may also seek power, excitement, and pleasure to manage shame. Obsessive pursuit of love is a defense for feeling unlovable. Love and romance addicts escape shameful feelings by spending hours fantasizing about an ideal relationship. We might pursue perfection to cope with shame: by getting repeated cosmetic surgeries, for example, or by compulsively dieting or exercising. We modify our outsides to soothe our insides. These efforts don't work, and we repeat the process because we're not addressing the root cause of our pain.

Addiction may start as an escape, but in time, our behaviors humiliate us and our relationships and work suffer. We become disappointed in ourselves, feel more out of control, and increase our addiction to deal with the negative feelings. In this downward negative spiral, we eventually feel helpless to limit or stop our addiction, and we instead promote the very feelings of shame and humiliation we were trying to avoid.

Horney's Coping Strategies

The techniques we use to cope with shame eventually begin to shape our personality. Karen Horney delineated three contrasting styles for coping with anxiety, shame, and hostility, each distinguished by neurotic needs. (See Table 3.1.) One approach is mastery, or to be an aggressor and move *against* people. Another strategy is freedom, or to be detached and move *away from* people. The third solution is love, or to be self-effacing and move *toward* people in compliance. In this section, I summarize her description of these three types and refer to them as the *Master*, the *Bystander*, and the *Accommodator*. Any coping method may rigidify into a personality type, but rarely are we

Table 3.1. **Karen Horney's Coping Strategies**[8]

Moves Against People—Aggression
• Need for power, control, and perfection
• Need to exploit others
• Need for social recognition and prestige
• Need for admiration
• Need for achievement
Moves Away from People—Detachment
• Need to restrict life
• Need for self-sufficiency
• Need for perfection
Moves Toward People—Compliance
• Need for affection and approval
• Need for a partner
• Need to restrict life

solely one type. We generally have characteristics of more than one type. Note that, to some extent, all of the needs in Table 3.1 are normal but become neurotic when they're compulsive and inappropriate or unrealistic. Many of them are typical of co-dependents, particularly those of the compliant Accommodator, who seeks to solve inner conflicts and pain through love.

The Master

The Master has an expansive personality and moves against people. This is an extroverted solution to shame. These individuals feel superior and seek mastery and control of their environment and others in order to get their needs met. They avoid feeling vulnerable and helpless at all costs, and some believe showing warmth or tenderness is equivalent to weakness, of which they're fearful and ashamed. Masters hold perfectionist, idealistic goals of prestige and power, which they pursue and fantasize about to avoid feeling inferior. By being powerful and superior, they protect themselves from feelings of self-doubt, unworthiness, guilt, and self-contempt. They accumulate symbols of power, success, and strength, such as a costly or powerful car, a trophy wife, or a mansion. They do these things to avoid taking responsibility for their feelings and behavior, which further alienates them from their real self.

Tim, a client of mine, exemplified this type of behavior. In the midst of a divorce, he entered therapy, disturbed that his wife couldn't accept his infidelity. The self-examination he had to undertake in therapy proved too much, as it made him more aware of his guilt and feelings of powerlessness. He soon quit therapy, claiming that it required him to face his weaknesses, and to be too open and vulnerable. This sort of self-examination threatened Tim's idealized self, which is incredibly difficult for the Master type.

Although not all Masters are openly hostile, they view the world as basically hostile and therefore move against people aggressively. Some may project their hostility onto others, justifying their own attitude and behavior. They express, rather than repress, their anger and attempt to exercise power over others, often by exploiting them to gain admiration, prestige, or recognition, even if it means being feared. Masters might subjugate others so as not to be subjugated the way they once were by a controlling parent. This may be expressed as machismo, bullying, or other forms of verbal and physical abuse.

Masters may appear calm, unresponsive, and in control, and may seem to have enviable competence and self-confidence; however, they're extremely dependent on success, prestige, and others' admiration and recognition to assuage their unconscious internalized shame, which is no less than that of other types. This makes them hypersensitive to criticism and humiliation, often perceiving it where none exists. They consciously or unconsciously dread being considered a fraud, failing, or having their shortcomings revealed, their opinions or authority questioned, or their self-esteem or pride tarnished. Should this happen, Masters can feel crushed and depressed. Some will unleash their rage and aggression to avoid feeling ashamed and empty.

Unlike self-effacing codependents who identify with their shamed, devalued self, many Masters are narcissists, who come to believe that they *are* their idealized self. Their sense of entitlement compensates for unconscious feelings of deprivation and inferiority, which surface when they don't get special privileges. Although they might appear to have high self-esteem and not need others, this isn't the case. Masters will charm people to win their admiration and might boast about themselves and their plans and accomplishments to avoid feeling shame or like a failure. Ordinary isn't good enough for Masters. As children they were not seen as separate from their parents, and this created an inner emptiness and unattainable need for attention, control, and recognition. The phrase, first declared by Cesare Borgia, "Either Caesar or nothing," states not only his grandiose goal, but also that not becoming Caesar would be unthinkable. He'd *be nothing* and unable to tolerate himself without the position and power of Caesar.[9]

Some Masters seek moral mastery and feel morally superior to others. Driven by shame, they compulsively strive to perfect themselves. They place a higher value on justice than mercy. In their mind, their success is due to their virtue, and they have no sympathy for the problems of others—nor themselves. When they suffer a serious misfortune, it can shatter the entire foundation of their personality.

The Bystander

This personality type has a resigned, detached attitude, being an observer rather than a participant in life. Bystanders construct a personality based on withdrawal, discussed earlier, so as not to need, want, or be hurt or disappointed. Their shame makes them feel unworthy of connection. Their solution to the problem of shame is to move away from people. They purposefully curtail life to have peace at any price and avoid the shame anxiety that comes with close relationships. By radically withdrawing, the pain of separation from others and the desire for intimacy and its accompanying anxiety tend to disappear.[10] Averse to effort, they don't compete, argue, strive after goals, or get involved with others. If a group or individual becomes too important to them, they withdraw their feelings in order to not get hurt.

Although Bystanders may marry, they often withdraw emotionally or sexually from their partner through addiction, work, time on the computer, masturbation, or other isolating activities. They may withhold cooperation, affection, sex, compliments, participation, or traits that they know their partner desires. A fantasy relationship without the friction of someone else's needs and wants can be more satisfying to the Bystander than a real one.

Bystanders are intensely self-sufficient and value their freedom above all. Thus, they're extremely sensitive to any dependency, coercion, pressure, or advice and put up walls to not need anyone or be influenced. Others' requests can feel like commands. If someone starts to depend on them or have expectations of them, they feel pressured and pull away. These rigid boundaries belie a weak sense of self, for sometimes Bystanders can't distinguish their own wants from others' wishes and can even resent being pressured into doing what they *wanted* to do. They may feel coerced by their own wants, which are soon felt as directives, and they rebel against themselves.

My client Jerry was a recovering drug addict. He resisted committing to a regular recovery meeting, scheduling regular appointments with me, or making plans to socialize with friends. Soon after scheduling something that he initially wanted to do, it felt to him like an obligation, and he would inevitably cancel. He took up gardening, thinking it would be a peaceful escape, only to abandon the idea when he began to experience internal pressure from the commitment itself. It became something that he *should* do, an obligation, which took the pleasure out of it.

Bystanders can be passive-aggressive, since they don't allow themselves to become angry or ruffled. They're caught in a conflict between pleasing others and maintaining their freedom; they may compromise by complying, while defying with passive resistance. Sometimes, they project their aggression and inner "shoulds" onto others, whom they must then resist. One variation of the Bystander is someone who lives a shallow, uncaring existence, appearing to participate in life but in reality merely adapting to others and going through the motions without any real commitment.

Outwardly, Bystanders may appear not to be codependent. However, their self-alienation, repression of feelings and needs, perfectionism, control, intimacy issues, dysfunctional boundaries, and reactivity to others are symptomatic of codependency, which in their case looks like "counter-dependency," or exaggerated independence. This is also a strategy used by many codependents who relish their freedom when they leave a painful, enmeshed relationship and are newly in recovery.

The Accommodator

Even though many Masters and Bystanders are codependent, Accommodators make up the majority of *self-identified* codependents. Those who are addicted to love, romance, or relationships closely resemble the stereotypical codependent. Love is the alchemical elixir they hope will magically transform their loneliness, unhappiness, and shame. Accommodators yearn for happiness and validation with one significant person with whom they can merge to finally achieve wholeness. They move toward people, believing that love and being liked will protect them from being hurt. They have intense needs to be wanted, accepted, supported, understood, needed, and loved. Their craving makes them as dependent on a relationship as other addicts are on a process or drug. To ensure that they're desired, needed, and not abandoned, codependents take care of others, please others, and put others' needs and feelings first. Their personality is passive, compliant, self-effacing, and accommodating. To be accepted, they display likable traits and hide their true feelings, repress their anger, and don't set boundaries. The discrepancy between their public and private selves reveals their shame and emptiness.

Unlike Masters, Accommodators favor a submissive role and avoid power. In many ways, these two types are opposites. Yet underneath, Accommodators repress an expansive side— their pride and their ambitious and competitive impulses. They might avoid competition, sabotage themselves professionally or when playing a game, and feel guilty should they actually win. Instead of feeling confident, they're more or less aware of feeling inferior, flawed, and guilty. They fear success and avoid recognition, preferring to be the adviser to the executive, the manager of the celebrity, or the "woman behind the man." They don't exercise authority in their own life and are uncomfortable in a position of authority. When put in a supervisory role, they often feel guilty being in charge and have great difficulty communicating expectations, criticism, or disappointment to those they oversee. To them, assertiveness feels unkind, setting limits feels rude, and making requests feels demanding. Their assertive voice sounds harsh to them, though it seems normal to others. Like Masters, Accommodators also might feel like a fraud when they're given more responsibility or receive praise or success.

Because love is the highest ideal, an Accommodator strives to be a loving, lovable, saintly, charitable, and selfless do-gooder—someone flawlessly noble and compassionate. Like Sister Luke, played by Audrey Hepburn in *The Nun's Story*, Accommodators constantly judge what they should do or should have done to live up to their ideal self-image, particularly relating to their highest values—being loving, unselfish, and attentive. They don't believe they have rights and feel guilty stating their needs, of which they're mostly unaware. This denial of self-interest and fear of conflict and abandonment makes setting boundaries extremely difficult for Accommodators, which allows others to easily abuse and exploit them. They have trouble saying "no," both to those who abuse them and to those who need them. They tend to self-sacrifice and go to any length to please. In order to do so, they deny, minimize, or rationalize abuse and hurt feelings, find fault in themselves, and try to be more understanding. This behavior is to prevent their greatest fear—rejection—which would dash their hope of finding lasting love and confirm their belief of being unlovable.

Accommodators suppress their anger and aggression to live up to their ideal and not jeopardize important relationships. This behavior makes them more vulnerable to shame.[11] They're afraid of abandonment, as well as their own and others' anger, because of what they witnessed in their childhood. "Don't make waves" is their motto. Though the type of abuse they experience may differ, Accommodators are usually reliving the experience of being shamed as a child, enacted by a partner whom they see as their parent. Emotionally trapped in their past, they're unable to access their power as an adult, further stunting their ability to assert and protect themselves and stop the abuse. Instead, to keep the peace, they placate, appease, and communicate indirectly in ways that are dishonest, manipulative, and passive-aggressive. Their aggression is directed at themselves and is expressed indirectly toward others through control, criticism, complaints, and passive manipulation.

Like other codependents, Accommodators have difficulty accepting responsibility for actions that might reflect negatively on them. Nevertheless, they frequently say "I'm sorry" to maintain an emotional connection. They stay in unhappy relationships because being alone would feel worse. They ignore not only their needs, but also their wants. Accommodators don't feel entitled to be happy, loved, successful, or worthy of pursuing their dreams, which can in turn cause them to feel like helpless victims. They don't realize their self-sacrificing behavior compounds their suffering, and any rage they might feel is masked by self-pity. "Why me?" externalizes their inner self-loathing and attracts sympathy. Shame denies Accommodators the power to change their lives. Long-term denial of their needs and anger can lead to bitterness, resentment, and depression and can result in psychosomatic symptoms and despair.

Exercises

Despite our defenses, we *are* able to heal our shame. In order to heal it, we have to consciously feel, and awareness is the first step in this process. Here are some suggestions to help make you more aware of your defenses and how shame can affect you:

1. Review the defenses against shame, and start paying attention to your own. Notice and track your defenses and when they occur. Don't judge yourself or worry about stopping them. For now, just become familiar with the ways you avoid feeling shame that aren't constructive. What defense do you use most often?

2. Consciously make an effort to not use that defense. Notice and write about what you feel. Be sure to comfort yourself if any negative feelings arise.

3. When you're critical, contemptuous, or arrogant (even silently) toward a person or group, write about what the person(s) did to evoke your criticism. Then pretend the object of your criticism was you by substituting "I" for the person(s), and read it aloud. Do any of your criticisms apply to you? Are you projecting your own self-criticism?

4. To respond to shame in healthy, assertive ways, compassion is required, not only toward yourself, but toward others, which means not using blame or aggression as a defense. Notice when you blame or rage at others, even silently to yourself. Write about the situation, and focus on your part in it. Make amends when necessary.

5. Write about feelings of envy. How does feeling envious make you feel about yourself? What's missing in your life, and what needs aren't being met? Create an action plan to meet these needs.

6. Which personality type(s)—the Master, the Bystander, or the Accommodator—do you feel most resembles you? Which specific traits do you relate to?

7. Write about the motives and ideals that drive your behavior.

This chapter has reviewed the many ways in which we avoid feeling shame by both putting up defenses and assuming one of three coping strategies. As painful as shame is, codependents try to avoid what underlies it at all costs. The following chapter looks deep into the bottom of the well of shame at emptiness, which everyone, not only codependents, wants to escape. You will learn ways to uncover and be with emptiness, which is the path to peace and wholeness.

Chapter 4

Emptiness: There's a Hole in My Bucket

I recently enjoyed an expansive, 180-degree view of the azure Pacific Ocean as the evening sun shone on golden ripples beneath a coral and turquoise sky. I felt tranquil, uplifted, and at one with life watching the tide ebb and flow while seagulls gathered on the shore. A few decades earlier, shortly after the death of my mother, this same scene filled me with tears of sadness, emptiness, and isolation. The vacant ocean mirrored the emptiness I felt internally. The relentless tide and far horizon added to my feelings of meaninglessness and despair. The brilliant sunset and carefree birds only intensified my alienation from life. Passersby shared pleasures and concerns, while I felt a robotic deadness.

It's not unusual to feel emptiness following a significant loss, such as divorce or the death of a loved one. Feelings of emptiness unaccompanied by grief, however, are often the underside of codependency and addiction. Emptiness lies at the bottom of the well of shame, which no one wants to feel. Being able to recognize it and learn to cope with it are valuable skills, because emptiness drives addictive behavior.

We may not be aware of our emptiness, particularly if we're out of touch with our feelings. In the absence of a significant loss, emptiness can result from prolonged exposure to abuse. It may be felt fleetingly or poignantly from living an "as if" inauthentic life. Emptiness can also rise to the surface of our well of shame; for example, if we live according to a narrowly prescribed role—either one that is culturally defined, such as a breadwinner or homemaker, or one we learned growing up, such as the family comedian or hero—we may feel empty when circumstances change, as in the event of an "empty nest" or unemployment. We feel empty and lost without a role to define us, because we're out of touch with our real, authentic self—our internal resource for strength, courage, and guidance.

Emptiness Defined

Emptiness is a vague feeling of unrest or restlessness that can take many forms. At its core is a basic anxiety. As my Pacific Ocean experience illustrates, emptiness stems from a very personal perspective. When I was feeling good about life, I took in the magnitude of the ocean's beauty. When I felt empty, the world reflected my feelings back to me. Regardless of the source of our emptiness, the experience of emptiness varies depending on our personality and the severity of any past or current trauma.

We each experience emptiness in our own unique way. It can often feel indistinct and indefinable. We might have a sense of not belonging, have a lack of answers, or feel that we as individuals, the work we do, and our lives are unimportant or lack meaning. We may feel we're "going through the motions" of life in a disconnected, mechanical manner. If we've denied our feelings for a long time, emptiness descends on us as nothingness—a vacuum, apathy, or boredom when we're alone. Accommodators feel emptiness when they're lonely or when they lack self-confidence. Masters and narcissists experience emptiness when their self-esteem isn't bolstered by aggression, power, or an active social life. Emptiness underlies a Master's grandiosity and an Accommodator's fear of abandonment.

Some people describe a hollowness in the pit of their stomach. Following a divorce, one woman I treated drew a picture of a raft floating at sea to portray her experience of feeling lost, adrift without bearings. The death of a loved one might also evoke the sense that not only the present but also the future is empty and meaningless because it's impossible to imagine life without the deceased. A surviving spouse may lose the internal mental or emotional functions that he or she depended on a partner to provide. Our emptiness is intensified when we feel lonely or disassociated.

Loneliness

Loneliness and emptiness are often felt together and considered two aspects of the same basic anxiety.[1] However, when we're lonely, we can also feel sad, miss someone, or have a desire to be with others. With emptiness, however, there's no longing and no feeling as if something is lacking. People who feel empty say they feel nothing and want nothing.

After losing his beloved Julie, poet Alphonse de LaMartine wrote, "I ask nothing of this immense universe."[2] His "indifferent soul knows neither charm nor joy," but contemplates the earth as a "wondering shadow," imagining being carried off in the wind like a "withered leaf."[3] After the death of her son, a client of mine named Martha described the emptiness that followed her initial sorrow as "not having enough blood in my veins."

Disassociation

Emptiness may also be accompanied by *disassociation*—a feeling of deadness, detachment, and lack of connection to self or reality. We may experience a floating sensation, nausea, dizziness, and mental and emotional numbness or feel as if the ground were slipping away. Disassociation doesn't happen to everyone. It typically occurs during a traumatic experience but can follow an acute shame attack. Unlike sadness, disassociation is a lack of feeling and a sense of emotional disconnectedness from life and others.

Existential Emptiness

The experience of emptiness unaccompanied by grief isn't unique to codependents. In the twentieth century, a group of philosophers came up with the concept of "existential emptiness." Many existentialists[4] view emptiness as a consequence of a lack of meaning and purpose, which is especially acute in modern times—not our parents' doing, as Karen Horney argued. These philosophers, psychologists, and social commentators maintain that, despite seeming to have everything, people who live in crowded cities, work at monotonous jobs, and are entertained by propaganda, advertising, and the media are actually leading shallow, discontented lives, alienated from nature, others, and their own true self.[5] When emptiness afflicts those who "have it all," the question becomes: What's the point of existence? A brief look at this phenomenon can help us identify whether our griefless emptiness is born out of living a lifestyle or in a society that lacks real meaning to us, or whether it's a symptom of codependency. However, differentiating between the two isn't always easy.

Many writers who call themselves existentialists don't view existential emptiness as primarily a psychological problem. To them, emptiness is a crisis of existence but not a mental disease.[6] The term *existentialism* was coined by philosopher Jean-Paul Sartre and grew out of post–World War II society. He described the nothingness and emptiness of living in a lonely universe, a sentiment expressed by numerous philosophers, writers, filmmakers, and artists of the twentieth century.

Sartre urged people to assume responsibility for making authentic choices and taking action in order to give meaning to their individual existence. For him the answer to emptiness was to live responsibly and authentically. He considered people-pleasing, or living a role to meet others' expectations, to be inauthentic and acting in "bad faith." Sartre was emphasizing the importance of the real self.

Psychological Emptiness

Whereas existential emptiness is concerned with our relationship to life and is considered more intellectual and spiritual, psychological emptiness is primarily concerned with our relationship with ourselves. Psychologists and psychoanalysts see emptiness as being rooted in childhood, not as a consequence of modern times.[7] The major difference is that psychological emptiness is accompanied by depression[8] and is deeply related to shame.

Depression includes a variety of symptoms, such as sadness, anxiety or restlessness, shame or unresolved guilt, apathy, fatigue, change in appetite or sleep habits, poor concentration, suicidal thoughts, and a void, or a hunger to fill the void. Most, if not all, codependents suffer from depression to one degree or another. It is ingrained in the self-alienation, isolation, and shame originating in childhood—referred to by psychiatrist James Masterson as *abandonment depression*.[9] For some of us, feelings of emptiness are constant; for others the feelings are felt periodically, vaguely or profoundly, and usually brought on by acute shame or loss. Meaninglessness can prevail over any sense of responsibility. If we've experienced trauma, we can feel as if we've fallen into a "devouring black hole," or like reality is broken.[10] Addicts and codependents often experience this type of depression when they stop using or end a relationship.

Sometimes emptiness and depression are also the consequence of our inability to be effective agents in our lives. As a result, we miss out on joy, contentment, self-love, and a sense of power. We keep ourselves from accessing our dreams, desires, and the energy of our real self, further reinforcing depression and confirming our belief that we can't direct our lives. We can feel trapped—that things will never change and that no one cares. All the while, we long to be cared for. (See Figure 4.1.)

When we're alone or shift from the stress and pressure of work to non-doing, we tend to quickly fill the emptiness before it has a chance to overtake us. We might obsess or fantasize about others, for example, or fill our head with negative thoughts that are driven by shame.[11] Our real self wouldn't treat us so poorly.

I once helped a client explore her emptiness while she was on sick leave. She complained that when she wasn't doing something useful, she felt empty and "worthless, like I don't have a right to be." She had to earn that right by being productive. She also felt guilty that she was burdening and possibly upsetting me if I thought about her between sessions or reacted sadly to something she talked about. Tearfully, she said she had to walk a fine line between being interesting enough to gain my attention and not causing me to react or care too much. She couldn't imagine that I might be interested in her, and insisted that my concern was strictly about her problems and not her as a person because she wasn't worthy of my interest.

Internalized shame can make us readily believe that our feelings of rejection and loneliness are because we're unworthy and unlovable. We personalize other people's actions and feelings and readily feel responsible and guilty, further lowering our self-esteem and increasing our shame. This perpetuates our assumption that if we were different or didn't make mistakes, we wouldn't have been abandoned or rejected. Shame also results in self-imposed isolation, which can compound our shame, depression, emptiness, and loneliness. This self-reinforcing, vicious circle is shown in Figure 4.1, although the feelings are in no particular order:

Figure 4.1
The Circle of Emptiness and Shame

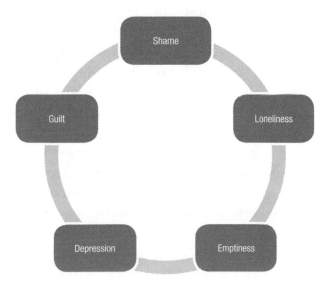

An Insatiable Hunger

Because we've lost touch with our real self, and our ideal self is unattainable, we become dependent on something outside of ourselves in an attempt to escape our emptiness. But it can neither be escaped nor filled, leaving us with an insatiable hunger—a craving.[12] What we crave varies, from material goods, sex, or mood-altering drugs to people.

Codependent Cravings

As codependents, without an external focus, we feel discontented and depressed because of our disconnection from our real self—our inner source of vitality. Some of us develop an insatiable need for validation, attention, understanding, or recognition. When no one meets these needs, we can feel anxious and empty, believing they will never be met. Feeling we have no other choice, we continue to attempt to fill the emptiness by living through or controlling others; turning to substance abuse or compulsive behaviors such as exercise, work, or sex; or distracting ourselves with other activities. If we're addicted to love, relationships, and romance, we look to others to provide motivation, companionship, and an escape from the emptiness. We may be drawn to drama-filled relationships to enliven us. We tend to consider stable people boring and are instead attracted to drug addicts, unavailable partners, dysfunctional work environments, excitement, abuse, or conflict.

Still, satisfying our craving for wholeness through distractions and addictions provides only temporary relief, while it further alienates us from our real self and avoids a real solution. This strategy stops working when the passion or the addictive high wanes, as it always does. We're then disappointed, our needs go unmet, and loneliness, emptiness, and depression return.

A lonely couple, longing for a passionate and vibrant relationship, may experience emptiness even when they're lying in bed next to each other. This can occur in relationships that lack emotional intimacy, become routine, or are laden with resentment after many years. In some marriages, parents may become overinvolved with their children, thereby filling the vacuum in their relationship that is devoid of closeness.

When we try to detach from an addictive relationship, when we're alone, or when we stop trying to help, pursue, or control another, our anxiety and emptiness can intensify. Although letting go and accepting our powerlessness over others is the first step in healing, it can evoke the same emptiness that addicts experience when giving up drugs or a process addiction.

Edward, a recovering alcoholic, wanted to leave his emotionally dull marriage to be with his mistress. He periodically struggled with sobriety and was grateful that his new relationship helped him maintain it. The mistress lived in another city, so he couldn't see her regularly, and it was during their separations that he yearned for her. He described his longing as a restless hunger. He desperately ached to be with her, despite his self-loathing about needing her so much and any suffering the affair might cause his family. As painful as the longing was, the buried emptiness and shame were worse. He felt like "a miserable, worthless failure," yet only felt like "himself" when he was with her. Gradually, he realized he was repeating the same addictive pattern to escape his anguish, only this time with an addiction to sex and romance instead of alcohol. And all his attempts to fill his emptiness only brought more shame.

Eating Disorders

Sometimes our emptiness is associated with an eating disorder. One woman explained that her bingeing filled her emptiness and the "deficiency" in her life.[13] It is believed that bulimia and anorexia are caused in part by spiritual emptiness felt as a "hunger of the soul" in people who have a "profound sense of disembodiment and lack of connection to their inner self and others."[14] They describe their body as an "empty vessel, devoid of life" that needs to be filled with comfort-giving food, which provides an illusion of control and authentic connection.[15] In recalling her own struggle, author Sandy Richardson names her all-encompassing emptiness a "soul hunger," and no matter how much she ate, the emptiness continued on its "vicious, gnawing path":

> *My eating disorder kept me safe. If I was just thin enough, pretty enough, maybe no one would look behind and see what a shameful, bad person I really was. The mask got heavier and heavier until I nearly collapsed under the strain of maintaining the lie. Once in treatment for my eating disorder, I discovered that dieting, food, and weight were not the issue. I was trying to fill a void that food could not possibly touch—a soul hunger.[16]*

Validation

Some people, particularly narcissists, have "intense stimulus hunger"[17] and need constant validation to escape their emptiness. When addicts stop one addiction (or tolerance dulls its effectiveness), they often add to it or replace it with another addictive behavior, as Edward described above. But this also doesn't address the underlying problem. Nothing satisfies what can become a biochemical need. After eating a wonderful meal, the writer Ernest Hemingway reflected:

> *. . . the feeling that had been like hunger when we were on the bridge was still there when we caught the bus home. It was there when we came in the room and after we had*

*gone to bed and made love in the dark, it was there. When
I woke with the windows open and the moonlight on the
roofs of the tall houses, it was there."*[18]

And later, when he gives up gambling on horse races:

*By then I knew that everything good and bad left an
emptiness when it stopped. But if it was bad, the emptiness filled up by itself. If it was good you could only fill it
by finding something better.*[19]

Facing the Void

*"It is by going down into the abyss that we recover the
treasures of life."* — Joseph Campbell

People regard feelings of emptiness and loneliness as distinct
from themselves, as if their inner void could be eradicated,
avoided, or filled, and they often spend their lives trying to do
so. This illusion perpetuates endless internal conflict. Whether
our emptiness is existential or psychological, the solution begins with facing the reality that emptiness is both inescapable
and unfillable from the outside. Fundamentally, addiction is an
escape from the real self, independence, and self-expression.[20]
We need to stop the cycle, which requires that we step outside
of our comfort zone long enough to choose a different path—a
path of recovery. It may not be easy at first, but being codependent is no picnic either. And, in recovery, there is a light at the
end of the tunnel. We stop escaping, get in touch with our real
self, and begin living fully and authentically.

Abstain

In recovery we learn to stop ourselves from escaping (doing
the same thing over and over again and expecting different

results—Einstein's definition of insanity) by abstaining—we stop using our drug of choice, whether it's a relationship, a substance, or a behavior. In doing so, we acknowledge our powerlessness over our addiction. This is Step One of the Twelve Steps.

During abstinence, feelings of depression, emptiness, and shame often surface. We codependents must acknowledge our powerlessness over the addict and other people. We're suddenly out of a job and have to deal with feelings of inadequacy, because we're no longer devoted to changing someone. We now have to face a lack of meaning in our lives—the void that was formerly filled by drama (mental and physical activity to control and manipulate another person)—just as the addict must face the loss of his or her drug of choice. For both partners, the emptiness that was masked by addiction is now revealed. It can be overwhelming when each acknowledges that he or she has an addiction, subject only to a daily reprieve their willpower can't control.[21] However, this powerful surge of feelings is temporary.

Accept and Detach

To allow our real self to emerge, we detach, letting go of our need to control others or the situation. To bring about this transformation, family therapist Thomas Fogarty recommends giving up all expectations of others and attempts to change them. The objective is to voluntarily experience the emptiness that occurs by *intentionally not trying to escape despair.* Abandon hope as well, he suggests, and allow a humbling powerlessness to occur. Fogarty believes this "forces a person to get something from himself and to get less from the outside. Paradoxically, *the less he tries to get from outside himself, the more he gets . . .* From this despair, in a strange way, comes a sense of self-esteem and self-respect."[22] (Emphasis is mine.) Confusion, restlessness, and depression result, which we must endure long enough, without reverting to old beliefs and patterns, to permit real change and acceptance. At this point, expectations are more aligned with reality, so that action, if required, is more constructive. This surrender of control requires courage—the courage to face our emptiness and accept our powerlessness. However, doing so is itself an act of faith, an affirmation of life and the real self.

In Twelve Step programs such as Alcoholics Anonymous (AA), Al-Anon, and Codependents Anonymous (CoDA), this surrender makes room for the Power greater than ourselves to come into our lives and help us restore our sanity (Step Two). In Step Three, we make the decision to turn our lives and will over to that Power, which doesn't mean passivity. Step Three helps us let go of anxiety and obsessive-compulsive thoughts and behavior associated with addiction, such as managing and controlling other people.

When we accept our powerlessness, we experience a major shift in consciousness back to our real selves. Awareness of separateness and responsibility for our own life arises. This is the beginning of change. In writing about food addiction, Geneen Roth recommends welcoming whatever is going on, hinting that there's a "whole universe"[23] to discover between emptiness and the act of filling it with food (or any other addiction). The task for us then becomes discovering and expressing our real self and pursuing authentic goals.

Assume Responsibility

If the deepest despair is the loss of our real self, the solution is to assume responsibility and choose to live authentically: to become our real self. Existentialists emphasize individual decision making and determination of values that require us to take risks and not be enslaved by convention, internal "shoulds," or fear of abandonment. Leading an authentic life is powerful medicine—it heals codependency and is the antidote for depression and emptiness. Both existentialists and Twelve Step programs urge action and personal accountability—living a moral life, taking a daily inventory, and making amends, all of which are covered in Steps Four through Ten of AA, Al-Anon, and CoDA.

When we assume responsibility for our life, we're challenged to take risks, but we must first discover our individual feelings, needs, and desires and then be able to honor them. Rollo May believes that if a human being is "not growing *toward* something, he does not merely stagnate; the pent-up potentialities turn into morbidity and despair, and eventually into destructive activities."[24]

Challenge Your Thoughts

Living authentically requires being able to experience the emotional pain that comes with detachment and letting go. Rather than get caught up in the story and drama of our relationship or our loved one's behavior, problems, or addiction, we can take time to be with our feelings, cravings, and codependent urges. We can allow ourselves to be still, observe, and welcome them, rather than react or fill our mind with obsession and worry. When we detach, we sit with the urge to react or to contact, help, or criticize someone, and we challenge our thoughts. We ask ourselves: *What has been the outcome of reacting or taking such action in the past? Beneath the fear, do I experience emptiness or loneliness? Can I continue one more day without trying to control or escape my own feelings?* When we become an observer, we give ourselves the space to realize that these fears and images are mental constructs; in and of themselves, they're empty. By embracing our emptiness, pain, and fears, we're connecting with our real self and invoking our own divinity. This is what makes life meaningful and exciting.

Meditate

Psychologist Carl Jung saw alcoholism as a spiritual problem. He wrote to Bill Wilson, cofounder of Alcoholic Anonymous, that alcoholism was "man's search for wholeness—an attempt to effect a union with God," which he believed was the solution.[25] Used wisely, the spiritual perspective adds an important and often overlooked dimension to approaching painful emotions. Meditation can be extremely useful for calming the mind and getting in touch with our spiritual side, which is closely linked to our real self. Step Eleven invites us to improve our conscious contact with our Higher Power through prayer and meditation. This can be an avenue to get acquainted with our feelings and true self.

By calming our mind through deep relaxation or meditation, we become more present and create a positive shift, even if only momentarily. When we go deeper in order to uncover erroneous beliefs and their emotional roots, we allow healing to occur. Trauma is physiological and lives inside the body. Although healing shame and trauma are not the focus of meditation, tracking sensation as it moves through the body can transmute these feelings into something else. It brings conscious awareness and often resurrects memories of prior ordeals, releasing pent-up energies around which the body-mind has constricted. We then experience more vitality and courage to devote to the present.

Meditation helps us move through painful emotions, but for some people, meditation is difficult. They're unable to meditate or be still on their own. Some of us use habitual defenses to prevent self-examination or use meditation to escape feelings or problems. Some people experience emotions or images that are too disorienting or frightening to tolerate. Still others become compulsive about meditation and strive to experience blissful states or perfect their ideal self, rather than accept their real self. The road to enlightenment can become an alluring but deceptive detour from facing our shame and low self-esteem.

If we're just starting a journey of recovery, we might be too anxious or afraid to deeply explore obsessions and distractions and the Pandora's Box of feelings that this process can unleash. This can be true even if we show a powerful, self-confident exterior. When we feel stuck with these feelings, we're wise to seek outside help through therapy.

Seek a Therapist

Many codependents are used to being self-reliant. However, when embarking on an expedition into uncharted territory, it makes sense to bring a companion. Being alone with our despair, shame, and emptiness for many days or months can cause us to re-experience emotional trauma from childhood. Connecting with an experienced guide helps to relax the fear and provide a sense of safety. Psychoanalyst Robert Stolorow emphasizes the importance of healing trauma in a safe environment that establishes a "relational home" to detoxify, understand, and integrate painful emotional states so that they're "less overwhelming and more bearable," enabling individuals to live more authentically.[26] Psychotherapy provides a method for approaching these states gradually in a secure environment. A nonjudgmental, experienced therapist, spiritual guide, or sponsor can provide an emotional holding space, a "relational home," where you can be with your pain in a way that's unlike what you experienced growing up. In a nonthreatening environment, you can examine and dis-identify with the voices and emotions that accompany states of severe shame and emptiness. To a lesser degree, group therapies or Twelve Step meetings like Al-Anon or CoDA can offer this as well, depending on the group members, nature of the material, and extent of the trauma.

Live Your Life

Although emptiness, shame, and trauma need to be addressed, balancing painful emotional states with healthy, life-affirming activity is equally important. Additionally, recovery includes taking risks, taking action, and learning to communicate authentically so that we can build a stronger self and a more meaningful life.

My experience is that there's no one-size-fits-all formula for working with emptiness, and the right approach varies depending on the strength of your core self, your personality, your degree of recovery, and the stability of your current life circumstances.

Exercises

If you feel ready to try meditation, there are numerous techniques, such as chanting and observing or counting breaths. I've outlined eight techniques elsewhere.[27] Below are a few suggestions.

Beyond Roth's approach, the Eastern teacher and philosopher Krishnamurti taught that it's an illusion to believe that we're separate from our emptiness and loneliness. Loneliness can only be understood, never escaped or overcome—except temporarily. He advocated *loving* difficult feelings of loneliness, emptiness, and sorrow by bringing intimate, one-pointed attention to them. This means to be in "direct communion" with suffering, without preconceived notions or objections.

To practice this, he suggested that we remove all barriers to being one with our experience, including thinking about it. His method requires the tricky realization that "I" the observer is in fact also empty. "I" can observe, but cannot act to change the emptiness. This awareness melts the illusion of separateness. He believed that once the split between you the observer and your experience disappears, fear, loneliness, emptiness, and sorrow will dissolve. When this happens, you will feel integrated, content, in a state of *aloneness,* where there is fullness and your mind is still and no longer seeking.[28] Thus, loneliness can be the doorway to aloneness, which in contrast, is not isolation. In aloneness, the mind feels no insufficiency and is creative and independent, neither resisting, reacting, nor in search of happiness or something outside itself.[29]

One useful meditation practice is to sit quietly in a comfortable position and ask yourself, "Who is thinking?" or to notice the discrepancy between your actions and your plans and intentions.[30] This is a powerful tool for cultivating mindfulness and self-awareness. The empty space allows us a "pause that refreshes," so we can be less reactive to our feelings and other people. Like refreshing a webpage, it awakens us from our habitual trance to provide a moment of choice in how we respond, rather than react.

Buddhists turn the concept of "emptiness" on its head. Rather than being a painful emotional state, it's a method to end pain and suffering and reach enlightenment. Here is another meditation technique, an instruction from twentieth-century Thai Buddhist teacher Ajahn Cha:[31]

> *Put a chair in the middle of a room.*
> *Sit in the chair.*
> *See who comes to visit.*

Many of us find it difficult to sit still and meditate. Some people avoid meditating because the "visitor" in Cha's technique is usually anxiety, shame, distress, or sleepiness, which, if not genuine fatigue, may itself be a defense mechanism. I highly recommend getting acquainted with these visitors, rather than trying to escape them through relationships, activity, and addiction. Be with them. Afterward, journal about your meditation experience. Include how you felt before, during, and after it.

This chapter has examined and distinguished various approaches to emptiness and ways of being with it. Hopefully these approaches have led you to become more aware of and perhaps explore the underpinnings of shame and addiction. In the next chapter, we will examine how shame and emptiness drive the major symptoms of codependency.

Chapter 5

Shame and Symptoms of Codependency

Emptiness is the deepest, darkest, and most pervasive of co-dependency symptoms. But shame and anxiety weave a common thread throughout a number of symptoms associated with codependency. In turn, these symptoms cause us to behave in some predictable ways. Many of them, such as perfectionism, denial, and caretaking, are also defenses to shame. Let's look at some of the most common symptoms—the thoughts and beliefs we have about ourselves that others don't see.

Impaired Self-Esteem

Whereas shame is a powerful emotion with physiological symptoms, self-esteem is a cognitive evaluation we make about ourselves. It's how we think about ourselves. Our destiny and success or failure are largely the result of our thoughts and self-esteem. Self-esteem impacts our relationships with others as well as our relationship with ourselves. It affects self-care, boundaries, and communication. Our self-esteem determines the way we allow others to talk to us and how we value and communicate our needs, thoughts, and feelings. It underpins our personal integrity and our ability to pursue life-affirming goals, make decisions, and be an effective parent. Low self-esteem is at the center of nearly all symptoms of codependency.

It's normal for us to feel good when we receive praise, acknowledgment, or compliments. But as codependents, when others try to boost our self-esteem, we may feel uncomfortable because internally we don't resonate with positive evaluations of ourselves. We might discount an achievement or question the motives or judgment of the person praising us. Even codependents who enjoy recognition can't sustain the good feelings because they don't really have "self" esteem. True, healthy self-esteem isn't dependent on success or others' love or approval, which could be called "other-esteem." True self-esteem comes from inside us—the good thoughts and beliefs we have about ourselves.

Healthy Self-Esteem

People with healthy self-esteem may feel down or disappointed when they have setbacks, but they're resilient and quickly recover. They don't usually take things personally, and they accept who they are despite their flaws, failures, and limitations. When they make mistakes, they're more self-forgiving and let go of self-judgment. Instead of comparing themselves to others, positively or negatively, they appreciate their singular individuality. They believe they're enough as they are, without feeling compelled to improve themselves.

Good self-esteem is different from inflated self-regard, which isn't healthy and is actually a defense to shame. Narcissistic and arrogant individuals who have an unrealistic, conceited view of themselves also tend to have impaired self-esteem, as we discussed in chapter 3. Healthy self-esteem means having accurate self-perceptions, accepting ourselves without shame as imperfect humans, with limitations and faults as well as talents and unique qualities. Healthy self-esteem means not having to camouflage our hidden shame with arrogance.

All the other symptoms of codependency reflect low self-esteem. The good news is that we can use some easy tools to improve self-esteem and address a lot of our symptoms. We'll learn about these tools later in the chapter. For now, let's look at some of the other symptoms of codependency and see if any of them feel familiar.

Self-Judgment

Self-judgment is not just a symptom of impaired self-esteem; it's a *major contributing cause* of it. Most of us aren't aware of how often we judge ourselves—our appearance, actions, conversations, thoughts, needs, and feelings.

We likely bombard ourselves daily with a "tyranny of the shoulds," first coined by Karen Horney.[1] The Critic reviews our appearance, behavior, personality, and conversations, looking for flaws and mistakes, which discourages us. The Critic tells us what we *should* or *shouldn't* have done, what we *should* or *shouldn't* do, and what we *should* or *shouldn't* think and feel. Often these "shoulds" are rigid and not based on the facts and variables of the events and people involved. Instead, they assume we can control people and outcomes. In other words, we don't consider that others make their own personal decisions or that many circumstances are beyond our control.

We're both persecutor and victim. The more we try to correct ourselves, the more our anxiety escalates. When we're full of anxiety, it's hard to have fun—we stifle spontaneity, play, and creativity. It's like having a resident spy constantly on the look-out for any false move to throw us into the shame dungeon. Instead of being solution-oriented, when we make a mistake or have a problem or negative emotions, our Critic goes on a fault-finding spree that makes it difficult to take appropriate action and creates more self-doubt and insecurity. Frequently, clients come to me feeling down for no apparent reason. After retracing their recent reactions to events, the culprit is inevitably the Critic and its judgments. Once clients examine and release the Critic's admonishments, their energy returns, their mood lifts, and their real self is free to enjoy the present.

The Critic generally doesn't discriminate among its victims. Blame and fault-finding can be internal, external, or both. A Critic may be critical of others in our lives, for example, especially those who are closest to us. This contributes to abusive communication, caretaking, and controlling behavior. If we project our Critic onto others, we become hypersensitive and may even turn a compliment into a criticism: "You look well" becomes "Did she think I looked bad before?" "Did you lose weight?" becomes "Did he think I looked fat before?" "You got an *A*!" is heard as doubt: "*You* got an *A*?" Codependents are particularly sensitive to others' setting boundaries because co-dependents themselves don't know how to set them. "I think I'll go now" means "I'm boring you" or "You don't like me." Self-criticism may be a thorn in our side, but it is also one of the first things we can change to improve our self-esteem.

Lack of Confidence

If we often doubt our thoughts and opinions, or are hesitant to share our opinions in a group, we may be lacking confidence. When we're used to accommodating and reacting to others, we become unsure of our own values, beliefs, and convictions, which encourages even more reliance on others. We may not like to take risks or make changes. Self-criticism and shame anxiety can prevent us from learning or trying something new. Getting easily overwhelmed when starting a project or easily discouraged while learning might mean that the task is too far beyond our skill level, but generally these are signs that we lack the confidence to succeed or accomplish the task. We foresee ourselves doing it poorly, failing, or looking foolish, which leads us to give up too soon.

Lack of Self-Trust

Self-trust is based on self-knowledge. How much we trust ourselves depends on how well we know our real self—our wants, needs, desires, values, and preferences. The real self, the place inside us that knows what's best for us, is where healthy people go to seek answers. Because we aren't well connected to our real self, we often feel uncertain and think about what we *should* do—what our ideal self would do. When we don't know what we need, we get confused and easily influenced by others. We have a hard time —and can even be paralyzed by—making decisions, and we're deathly afraid of making mistakes. Consequently, we look to others for validation, opinions, and answers, which creates even more distance from our real self and hinders the growth of self-trust.

Rather than responding to what we want and need, we think about what we *should* do—what our ideal self would do. This internal conflict is heightened when someone—a wife, for example—is conflicted between two "shoulds": being "the dutiful daughter" and attending her parent's birthday party or being "the dutiful wife" and staying home with her sick husband. The inner conflict is heightened by the "shoulds" of her parents and husband. At first, there's no sense of "I" in the decision-making process. But she has to make a decision, and she makes progress toward building self-trust when she struggles between what she wants to do, what she perceives she *should* do, and what others want from her. Sorting this out isn't easy, but growth happens in the process, giving her the opportunity to make a conscious choice. Deciding to go to the party, stay home with her husband, or do neither (go to a movie with a friend so she gets a needed break, for example) can all be healthy choices, as long as she considers her needs and wants when making the decision.

Our trust pendulum can swing from one extreme to the other. Just as we don't trust ourselves, we can distrust others. We may trust untrustworthy people, or view others through the lens of a hostile, early home environment, which can promote a sense of defenselessness in a potentially dangerous world. Or, we might trust those who appear to provide approval, love, or protection way too easily. Because we deny our own perceptions and feelings or don't trust them, we handicap our ability to accurately assess people and circumstances.

Feeling Unimportant

Many codependents don't feel entitled to have their wants or needs met, to be happy, loved, or successful. We may believe that we're a burden to others and anticipate the shame of having our requests criticized or refused. When we do speak up, we may easily back down because someone or something else is more persuasive or seems more important, or because we believe that we're being selfish, demanding, or needy.

Low self-worth and shame may open the door for others to take advantage of us or be abusive. I've worked with clients with life-threatening illnesses whose only concern was how it affected their children, as if their own life didn't matter to them. Usually, however, they're only conscious of their belief that they don't matter *to others.* This is a chief complaint that couples make—that they have no impact on their partner, and that their voice and needs don't matter. But the truth is that codependents voluntarily put others first and give up their own needs and rights, which they deny or ignore. Other times they complain, but don't take steps that would improve their lives.

Figure 5.1

Symptoms of Codependency

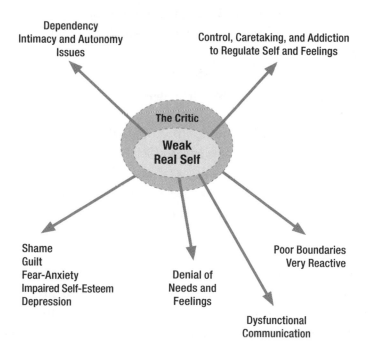

Shame-Related Emotions

We've discussed a number of feelings and emotions associated with shame, such as worthlessness, fear, arrogance, anger, and envy. But anxiety, guilt, and depression are also common among codependents and deserve further attention.

Anxiety

Most codependents live with anxiety. I'm not referring to the real fears of living with an abuser, alcoholic, or drug addict, but fears generated from shame anxiety—the anticipation of experiencing shame and abandonment, just as we did as children. The need to be loved and accepted can make us hypersensitive to any sign of disapproval or abandonment. We're anxious about rejection, abandonment, or making a mistake, and even about being successful. We might cling to people who are disapproving or rejecting, which can perpetuate and reinforce our anxiety and shame. Anxiety can drive us to worry about what we said or did, fret about what we will say or do, or endlessly come up with hidden meanings about other people's motives and reactions.

When we uncover and heal our original shame, we release our shame anxiety and free our real self. This allows our internal battle to subside and increases our self-awareness, which prepares us to stand up to danger. As our inner strength grows, the world appears less threatening, and our anxiety wanes.

Guilt

Guilt about the past and present can plague us just as much as anxiety about the future. Typically, this guilt is prompted by our deeply buried shame; therefore, unlike healthy guilt, it paralyzes us from doing anything about the situations that are causing the guilt. We feel guilty when we don't measure up to the "shoulds" attached to our ideal self. Those of us who are Accommodators experience guilt about feelings such as anger or jealousy that are in conflict with our ideal of goodness, or we feel guilty when we move toward autonomy because we might risk disapproval and abandonment. When our needs conflict with those of others, we may feel too selfish and guilty to assert ourselves. We feel guilty for other people's feelings and readily try to accommodate or accept responsibility for them. This makes it difficult for us to set boundaries, but when we do set them, guilt follows as surely as night follows day. We're constantly apologizing and feel guilty for not being better or doing more. Sometimes we admit our guilt in an attempt to pacify another's feelings. This is not the same as taking responsibility for our actions; its' a way of avoiding the deeper shame we would feel if we did take responsibility. In this way, guilt is not only caused by shame, but it is also used to defend against it.

Bystanders suffer conflicting "shoulds" of their inner Critic. Their inner dictum to guard their freedom at all costs conflicts with what they think they should do, or what others want them to do. Even doing something as beneficial or routine as taking a walk, a nap, or a shower can become a "should" that must be resisted. This resistance simultaneously causes guilt, which creates perpetual inner conflict.

Masters, on the other hand, are less likely to be bothered by guilt. They feel guilty when they think they're not doing enough to meet their own standards of success and perfection or when they go too far to get their way. However, they more often use blame or projection to make others feel guilty rather than take responsibility. When they do take it, they quickly let it go.

Depression

> *"The most common form of despair is not being who*
> *you are."* — Søren Kierkegaard

Prolonged self-alienation, neglect of our needs, and exposure to shame can lead to depression, which is commonly experienced by codependents, particularly by women. This may be because women often blame themselves for their failures and blame external circumstances for their successes, while men tend to do the reverse.[2] Depression can result in a numbing of feelings due to the repression of emotions, particularly anger and shame. Many of us feel a mild depression that goes unnoticed as long as we're distracted by activities, caretaking, or troubled relationships. Relationship problems can provide a perpetual reason to feel unhappy, but more unsettling is when everything is working in life, yet we have a vague sense of purposelessness. We eventually feel our resources and vitality depleting. By getting insights into where our shame comes from—including working through some of the exercises in this book—seeking professional help when self-help isn't enough, and getting involved in a recovery program, we can counter the shame and send depression on its merry way.

Denial of Needs, Feelings, and Wants

Most everyone uses denial at some point or another. It's a necessary defense that helps us cope. Whether it's dysfunctional and a symptom of codependency depends on how frequently we use denial and the impact it has on us and our lives and relationships. Many of us deny our own addiction or the addiction of those we love. Facing this harsh reality can cause shame as well as anxiety about the life-altering changes that would be necessary in order to make a real change. On the other hand, using denial as a coping mechanism over time leads to more secrecy, isolation, shame, and a progression of the disease— taking us farther and farther away from healing.

Some of us deny our current feelings and needs because in our childhood they were shame-bound. If our feelings weren't honored, we stopped expressing them and eventually may have stopped feeling them to the point that we still may have trouble feeling or identifying emotions as an adult.

Feelings are raw information—the data that give us clues that our needs are or aren't being met. That's how important feelings are. Denying or dismissing them is a major cause of our unhappiness—a major barrier to connecting with our real self. There are several levels of denial:

- Rationalizing, judging, or minimizing present feelings or needs

- Being unaware of present feelings or needs

- Being unaware of past feelings or events that are informing the present

- Being unaware of past shaming of needs or feelings

As codependents, we won't know about our shame-bound needs. We've either repressed them and learned to go without or don't feel entitled to have them met in the first place. However, we aren't truly as self-sufficient as we think, because denial doesn't in any way diminish the need; it only diminishes our sense of deprivation.

Masters don't want to be weak or needy but nevertheless expect others to meet many of their needs. Accommodators are often happy to oblige, because they devalue their own needs and desires, relative to those of others. For Accommodators, meeting their own needs violates the dictates of their selfless ideal. They fulfill other people's needs in the unconscious hope that others will reciprocate and fulfill their needs, only to become resentful when it doesn't happen. Some of us are direct about expecting someone—another codependent caretaker, typically—to fulfill all our emotional, and sometimes material and financial, needs. If we fall into this category, we can learn to meet the needs that we're capable of fulfilling ourselves.

For example, if comfort and nurturing were withheld and shame-bound in childhood, person A as an adult might not recognize when he or she needs them, or feel too ashamed to ask for them. It's likely that A is incapable of any self-nurturing, adding to his or her distress. Instead, this person might become moody, distant, or argumentative when nurturing is lacking. If aware of his or her need, A might self-soothe with an addiction or feel resentful and think person B should have figured this out and fulfilled the need. It might also be true that person A chose to be with person B, who is withholding, because the relationship is reminiscent of person A's childhood. With some recovery, A learns to meet his or her needs and also directly ask for specific help. If B persists in withholding, A might seek help elsewhere or leave the relationship.

Even though we can't usually recognize shame-bound feelings, denying them can have grave consequences. They can produce psychosomatic symptoms, such as fatigue or pain, or lead to dangerous or self-sabotaging behavior. If we deny that we feel fear, we might engage in risky behavior. For example, people who cut themselves compulsively are using physical pain to express the emotional pain that they're denying. Those of us drawn to argue (or argumentative people) or to behave passive-aggressively are most likely denying deeper anger.

Feelings provide a natural, internal guidance system that communicates feedback about the environment to know what is safe and what isn't, what feels good and what doesn't. Co-dependents with internalized shame who deny their feelings are unable to protect themselves and may not even know they're being abused, for example. They might believe seduction, false promises, and lies, or blame rather than trust their own dis-comfort, anger, or fear. Some who have been abused might be-come attracted to an abuser because they confuse fear with excitement.

Awareness of Needs and Feelings

If we want our needs to be met, we have to be aware of them. Awareness of feelings and needs includes being able to name them. This is an important part of healing that enables us to cope with emotions, meet our needs, and communicate both effectively. Even codependents who are aware of their feelings and needs can have difficulty expressing them directly.

If we're unable to identify our needs and feelings, and if we're unwilling to be vulnerable and disclose them, we will have a hard time resolving our conflicts. Often couples argue about the wrong things because they're unable to identify and request the specific need that they want met. For example, rather than admit her real feelings—even to herself—a wife who is feeling hurt and lonely might angrily blame her husband for spend-ing too much time on the computer, which pushes him further away. Repression of past feelings can also compound conflict. As a child, the wife may have felt ignored, and her husband is stimulating her deep abandonment pain. If she becomes ag-gressive in an attempt to hide it, he might feel afraid or angry or intentionally avoid her because her behavior reminds him of his childhood abuse, even though he isn't consciously aware of his past feelings. Healing the past trauma would make them both less reactive to each other.

Sometimes, we unintentionally bring our suppressed or re-pressed needs and feelings to our awareness through our own efforts. We may push people away in order to feel rejection, en-gage in dangerous activities to feel fear, provoke arguments to feel angry, indiscreetly expose ourselves to feel shame, partici-pate in illicit sex to feel excitement, or watch melodramas to feel sadness.

Once we can actually name our needs, we need to be care-ful not to judge them. We're likely to question them and think we shouldn't feel them. "E-motion" is meant to *move* us. If we judge our feelings, we don't allow them to flow and be released.

Perfectionism

It's possible to have high standards and goals without being a perfectionist. We might call it behavior excellence or even hard work. Perfectionism has a rigid, compulsive quality to it and is accompanied by damaging self-judgment. For codependents, perfectionism exemplifies a core belief that we're not good enough to be accepted by others. Being "average" feels inferior and anything less than "perfect" reflects how flawed we feel. Codependent perfectionists tend to compulsively aim to be-come their unattainable ideal self, unconsciously trying to be more acceptable to others.[3] They seek perfection in order to feel worthwhile, taking credit for what goes right and hiding their mistakes when something goes wrong. In the process, they des-perately resist making themselves vulnerable, or being human.

This impossible quest compensates for our buried shame. Yet the standard is impossible for us to achieve, and so our at-tempts to reach it continually fail. Chasing perfection supplies the Critic with evidence of the perfectionist's inferiority, de-fectiveness, and guilt. There is no middle ground or room for error. The perfectionist is either good or bad, a success or a failure. Perfectionists live under constant pressure to escape the Critic's judgment, which they project, convincing them that others might also judge and reject them. The Critic's verdict confirms what it already believes—that they're inadequate. A guilt-ridden, perfectionist accountant once joked, "I've only made one mistake—thinking I'd made one."

Parents encourage perfectionism when they overcorrect children, pressure them to excel, or only approve of them based on their performance. This behavior differs from accepting and acknowledging children's discouragement and sense of failure when they make mistakes, which helps them accept themselves and try again. It's beneficial to teach children to set realistic, achievable goals, based on their capacity and level of performance, and to acknowledge their progress as each step toward their goal is reached.

Perfectionists dread failure, and may even quit a difficult project to avoid failing. Learning or creating something new is difficult for them because the Critic blocks learning and creativity by judging early efforts. When perfectionists quit, struggle, fail, or even make a mistake, they generate self-recriminations that can spin them into shame and depression. And when they do achieve their goal, they often diminish its importance. A perfectionist can feel more relief than satisfaction upon receiving a perfect score. An "A" student might focus on the teacher's comments or wrong answers on an exam or minimize an honor by attributing it to luck rather than hard work or talent.

Jacqueline, an eminent scholar, told me that she attributed her success to her father because each time she published a book, he praised her but added that perhaps her next book should be more understandable, get more attention, and so on. Because of this, she was compelled to keep publishing and improving her writing. The root of the word *improve* is "to prove." She was trying to prove she was worthy of his approval—that she was acceptable. The sad result was that, after a noteworthy career, she could take no pride or satisfaction in her accomplishments. She could never do enough to please her father, so she found herself feeling deficient and unfulfilled.

Perfectionism can have serious consequences. The anxiety and shame it produces has been linked to depression, anorexia, and suicide.[4] It can also ruin relationships. Perfectionists may extend their perfectionism to their appearance, work, home, and family. Things must be in place, and their spouse and children must do their best—according to the perfectionist. The perfectionist can't accept differences in others. Perfectionists either negatively compare themselves to others or judge others against their idealistic standards. They may even become competitive and undermine their partner's efforts or successes. When their self-criticism is externalized, others feel anxious, unappreciated, and unacceptable.

Dependency

As children, we learn to be independent when our parents are willing to trust us and give up their control over us. Parents also need to support a child's sense of separateness and uniqueness, including individual thoughts, feelings, and needs. When a child's individuality isn't encouraged, he or she can develop dependent tendencies. If our parents were codependent, they were limited by their unmet emotional needs and lack of individuation. Directly or indirectly, they may have failed to support our separateness. Some parents look to their children for mirroring and validation, self-esteem, comfort, and/or companionship that they may not have received from their own parents. Some resist their child's efforts to set boundaries and spread his or her wings by being overprotective and over-possessive.[5]

They criticize their child's ideas, tastes, friends, career, religious choices, and lifestyle, compromising his or her budding sense of self.[6]

Moreover, codependent parents might not support their children's independence during key developmental stages, such as the separation of toddlerhood, when three-year-olds explore the world apart from their mothers, and adolescence, when teens challenge their parents in order to establish autonomy. If a parent's own abandonment issues are triggered—for example, when their youngsters start school or teenagers prepare to leave home—they may have difficulty letting go. They might use guilt to undermine their children's independence, with phrases such as, "You always do what *you* want," "I wish you wouldn't do this to me," "You don't care about me," or "You only think of yourself." Parental dependency on their children can often be exaggerated following a divorce, or when intimacy is lacking between the parents in a marriage.

Children who are not encouraged to become independent can suffer from a basic insecurity that impairs their ability to fully function as adults. Although on the outside codependents may appear to be successful and functioning exceedingly well, they're dependent on others' approval to feel worthy and lovable. This dependency on others for motivation, validation, and answers diminishes their self-determination.

Although Masters have a fair amount of motivation, most codependents are passive—which doesn't mean inactive. Rather, there is a sense of not being the author and director of our own life. We lack the capacity to want and to will action on our own behalf; we need others to incentivize or support us. Instead of initiating, we react. Our actions originate in others' expectations, feelings, and needs or from our internalized ideal of how we should be. It might be the expectations or needs of our partner,

child, friend, group, or authority figure, such as a teacher or su-
pervisor. Left to our own devices, we lack motivation. Instead
of making constructive plans and taking self-directed action,
we daydream, make excuses, scoff at our own ideas, or feel incapable of achieving them. We may have little impetus to seek
out pleasurable activities unless they're shared with someone
else. Otherwise, we don't enjoy them and won't experiment on
our own.

All addicts spend time thinking about, planning, and managing the object of their addiction. We can spend a lot of energy
thinking about or trying to understand or influence another
person. In the process, we give up our own interests, needs, and
goals. Accommodators in particular may completely adapt to
their partner, lose interest in their own friends and activities,
and even adopt pursuits and tastes they formerly disliked. They
may assume the lifestyle, views, and opinions of their spouse to
the extent that they see the world and others, including friends
and relatives, only through his or her eyes. In exchange for security, they abandon their real self and create more unhappiness and despair.

Codependents often feel trapped in unhappy relationships.
We may be fiercely loyal to an abuser and stay married because being alone would feel worse. Some of us are afraid to live
alone, and never have. Others fear no one else will love or accept them. On one hand, we crave freedom and independence;
on the other hand, we want the security of a relationship—even
a bad one. We're afraid to leave an unhappy relationship because our attachment need is so great. Most of us aren't aware
of this need. Even if we are, rather than leave, we rationalize our
situation and continue to sacrifice ourselves, or we fruitlessly
try to change the person we're with. Accommodators often
blame themselves for their unhappy predicament and believe

they should be more loving and understanding to make their partner love them. They believe in love, and that they have the power to make the relationship work. They try to change their partner or try to change themselves to become the person their partner wants. By trying to win the love their unavailable parent didn't give them, they may be unconsciously trying to heal the pain of their early childhood in an adult relationship.

When a relationship ends for the Accommodator, it often triggers a shame spiral. Normal grieving is compounded by shame-bound guilt and exaggerated feelings of rejection. It may take years to rebound from a breakup and longer than average, if ever, to recover from a divorce or a loved one's death.

Dependency also applies to those, including Masters and narcissists, who, although they may be able to pursue their own goals and self-interest, are equally dependent on their close relationships to confirm their inflated self-opinion, to prove themselves, and to ward off underlying shame. They may make monetary concessions to appease a partner but be abusive or argumentative or maintain an emotional or physical distance. These behaviors are used to manage their ambivalence about their dependency.

Control

To contain uncomfortable feelings, codependents attempt to control people, their environment, and their own emotions. We try to change other people's behaviors and feelings to feel better inside and to avoid our own shame. The greater our shame and emptiness, the greater our anxiety and need to control. We also control others because we're dependent on them. Due to our external focus, we see others as the cause of our problems, the solution to them, or both. When we're not blaming others, we blame ourselves, but this self-shaming differs from taking responsibility and rarely leads to corrective action, which may include getting help. Our success in controlling someone else is short-lived, and rather than solving the problem, it breeds resentment. Almost any behavior can be used to manipulate or control others and our environment. Anger, blame, demands, and abuse are the more obvious examples. Other methods include silence and talking too much, as well as seduction, isolation, favors, and withholding attention, money, or sex. One form of passive control is the codependent version of caretaking, and it can be fairly manipulative.

Caretaking

Codependent caretaking, in contrast to genuine caregiving, stems from shame. It feeds our self-esteem and pride, allowing us to hide our needs, our feelings, and the flaws we're ashamed to reveal. This caretaking includes not only gift-giving and other types of physical or financial help but also attending to others' emotional needs by listening, advising, solving their problems, and accommodating their requests. These sound like wonderful attributes, and they can be, provided the giver is not expecting anything in return, such as changed behavior.

Codependent caretaking is giving in order to get love. The motive is "I'll help you so you'll love and accept me." However, we still have needs, often unconscious, that we want fulfilled, which is why there are strings attached to caretaking. We take care of others, please, and self-sacrifice to ensure that we're needed, loved, and won't be abandoned.

As caretakers, we may take responsibility for more than 50 percent of the relationship. We relinquish self-responsibility and at the same time take responsibility for our partner's happiness, feelings, needs, expectations, and even his or her actions and problems. We may go to great lengths to be needed—by volunteering, doing more than our share of work on the job, and saying yes to unreasonable requests. We give more than is required because we don't feel valued or lovable unless we do. We make ourselves indispensable to ensure that we won't be fired. Helping others can become an obsession and compulsion, to the point where we can't say no to a request or listen to someone's problem without offering advice or help. We may even offer unsolicited advice or help when it's not wanted. However, our giving is laced with control and expectations. We expect gratitude, love, and acknowledgment and that the recipient of our advice will listen to us and change. If he or she does not, we feel unappreciated and resentful.

When someone we love is in the throes of addiction, our caretaking and desire to control can escalate. It's natural for us to worry about the addict and become preoccupied with his or her problems and addiction. The addict's erratic, irresponsible, and self-destructive behaviors feed our obsession, and we become increasingly frustrated, angry, and desperate. As our efforts intensify, even a parent truly motivated by love may blame and judge and try to reform the addict to avoid deeper feelings of pain and inadequacy. Meanwhile, our thinking and behavior can become more and more impaired, to the point where life becomes unmanageable, and our shame increases. At the end of the day, all of our efforts to help only heap more shame on the addict and provide welcome justification for the addict to blame and abuse us and continue his or her addiction.

Enabling

Enabling is a special category of caretaking and control. The term originally described those relatives of alcoholics and drug addicts who help their addicted loved one by removing the consequences of his or her behavior. For example, a wife might call in sick, making excuses for her hungover husband, or parents might repeatedly bail their son out of jail or give their daughter money even though they know she will spend it on drugs. This behavior prolongs the addiction and prevents the addict from experiencing the consequences of addiction, reaching out for help, and finding sobriety or abstinence. Without support, the enablers' fear and mistaken sense of responsibility for the addict's problems forces them to act even when they know better. The term *enabling* can be applied to any form of help that removes the natural consequences of someone else's behavior.

We attempt to control in order to avoid taking responsibility for our feelings, our actions, and the unmet needs that cause us unhappiness. We either adjust to others or think others should adjust to us. This is an unconscious, compulsive process that differs from acceptance, self-care, and healthy compromise, which are necessary in relationships.

Exercises

Here are some suggestions to help you discover how shame affects your thinking and behavior. For some of them, you will need your notebook or journal.

1. To heighten your self-awareness, list your "shoulds" for you and your family.

2. Practice replacing "should" with "prefer" when you talk to yourself and others. The first difference you will notice is that when speaking to others, the sentence begins with "I" not "You." This is an important step in taking

responsibility for your wishes. Notice how this change makes you feel.

3. Each time you're self-critical, give yourself a signal, such as snapping your fingers. Even better, give yourself a loving gesture, such as touching your heart or patting your shoulder. Include "shoulds" as self-criticisms.

4. List the codependent symptoms and behaviors that you can relate to.[7]

5. Do you try to get someone's approval or acceptance by sacrificing your needs or wants, not setting boundaries, or trying to impress or please him or her? Think this through and write down a few examples.

6. Take some time to make a list of *your* values, such as family, health, or hard work. Be careful not to let other people's values creep into your list. Meditate about what is most important to you. List at least twenty values. Does your life reflect your values?

7. Think of at least one thing you did for someone this week. Did your words and actions match your values, thoughts, and feelings? If not, what were your motives behind these words and actions? What beliefs were they based on? For example, my motive is: "I paid for my friend's meal so she would like me." My belief is: "She wouldn't be my friend if I were myself, because I'm not enough to be liked and loved."

8. Notice when you compare yourself more or less favorably to others. Is your Critic judging you or others?

9. Notice if you stop yourself from taking action on your own. Try taking action anyway, and write about your feelings and what they remind you of.

In this chapter, we have looked at how shame is interwoven with codependency. In the following chapter, we will consider how shame and codependent symptoms can create problems in our relationships.

Chapter 6

Love's Silent Killer

Relationships can be one of our greatest blessings and, at the same time, one of the most difficult aspects of our life. Relationships are meant to be more than companionship. They're a way for us to learn about ourselves, they give us an opportunity to recognize and heal our shame, and they support us in achieving our goals. Shame of course gets in the way, from the moment we select a partner, and it prevents us from enjoying a healthy relationship. To complicate things even further, we're often dealing not only with our own shame but with our partner's as well.

Shame has been called "the antithesis of love"[1] because it sabotages our best efforts in a relationship. Shame tends to undermine all of the behaviors needed for a healthy relationship and prevents many of us from developing the necessary skills. To feel deserving of love, we need autonomy and a healthy sense of self-worth. To communicate openly and honestly, and to give of ourselves without creating barriers, we need to know how we feel and know we're in the relationship for the right reasons.

Some of us see love as the solution to shame and a loving partner as a means to feeling complete. By seeking wholeness through someone else, we necessarily become dependent, just like addicts who turn to drugs to fill their emptiness. The hunger and emptiness we feel inside makes us cling to relationships, even abusive ones. These addictive relationships are based not on love but on escapism, for love cannot abide with dependency or emptiness.[2] They lead to control, jealousy, fear, and anger.

Shame invites a host of destructive behaviors and beliefs to the relationship. We use manipulation and control to allay our fears. We take responsibility for our partner's behavior and life while neglecting our own. And we unconsciously deploy defenses to prevent intimacy, since closeness would most surely expose our every inadequacy and risk rejection. Our dependency magnifies our fears and escalates our defenses.

While shame can destroy love, it can also be a path to healing. Many psychologists believe that people unconsciously select a partner reminiscent of a parent in order to reproduce a familiar, early parental bond and that we then use our shame to re-create unhappiness and trauma. These dysfunctional adult relationships then become opportunities for growth and healing.

I think it's safe to say that most codependents didn't witness many healthy relationships as children, and that many of their adult friends may be divorced or in unhappy relationships. They wonder what's "normal." Loving, healthy relationships require the qualities shown on the left in Table 6.1.

Self-Esteem in Relationships

Because we need to be seen as we see ourselves, we attract what we project, and so healthy self-esteem is essential to attracting and maintaining healthy relationships. If we have low self-esteem, and see ourselves as "less than," we're likely to attract a

Table 6.1. **Healthy and Dysfunctional Relationships**

In healthy relationships, partners:	In dysfunctional relationships, one or both partners:
give and receive love	withhold or reject love
feel worthy and lovable	feel inadequate, unlovable, or superior
openly communicate	feel defensive, uncommunicative, secretive
feel safe and trust each other	feel unsafe, unreliable, untrustworthy
are autonomous and interdependent	are dependent or needy, or avoid intimacy
respect flexible boundaries	lack separateness, have merged or rigid boundaries
accept differences	judge, reject, control
cooperate and compromise	are selfish, rigid, controlling
are assertive	are manipulative, abusive, indirect, disrespectful
listen and understand	ignore, dismiss, misinterpret
are reliable	are unreliable

partner who sees us the same way—and we will invite dysfunction into our lives.

The reverse is also true. Being seen by others as more powerful or better than our self-concept can provoke intense anxiety in us.[3] Receiving praise and positive feedback can make us so uncomfortable that we may unconsciously try to push away anything that challenges our negative beliefs—even love.

If we have low self-esteem, then we're likely to be drawn to someone who is unavailable, who depends on us, or who treats us as though we're unworthy of love and respect—just as we treat ourselves. We can only receive as much love as we feel we deserve, and we find it difficult to believe we're loved when we feel unlovable. We might acknowledge being loved for our success or looks, but not for our real self ("If he/she really knew me . . .").

We employ not only our trusty shame defenses, but defenses similar to those that our parents used to deflect affection, real acknowledgment, and tenderness.[4] We often hear or infer criticism where none exists. We project and then react to our inner Critic, who we believe is talking through our partner, which triggers shame and confirms our inner reality and our Critic's programmed beliefs about us. If our partner shows kindness, thoughtfulness, or affection, we may misinterpret or not even notice it, or we may distrust our partner's motives. We expect and may provoke our partner to treat us in accordance with our own negative self-assessments. We might unintentionally incite attacks that make us feel victimized. Some of us might goad our partner into withdrawing or rejecting us through endless complaints or requests for love that in the end prove that we're unlovable. Although a couple's behavior may be unkind or even cruel, the emotional bond they share feels familiar and comforting. This is especially true for codependents, who hold on to a romantic belief or rationalization that they're loved in order to alleviate the deeper fear of being unlovable. Meanwhile, shame causes patterns in our relationship that continue to reinforce and lower our self-esteem.

A former client of mine, Kent, insisted that his wife comply with all of his demands in order to prove to himself that he held the power in the relationship. This unconscious attempt to boost his self-esteem aroused the same feelings of powerlessness in her that he had about himself from his abusive childhood. His wife would often "forget" or comply half-heartedly, which enraged him. Kent's anger increased with his wife's passive-aggressive noncompliance and growing withdrawal, proving his original belief that he was weak and helpless. For Kent, like many codependents, his shame defense eventually confirmed the existing beliefs he had about himself. His emotional abuse had the effect of transferring his shame to her, triggering her defense of withdrawal.

Our Critic can also project onto loved ones the qualities and behavior that we dislike in ourselves or our parents. Finding fault with our partner preserves our own self-image from the Critic's judgment. We may take on a superior attitude in the form of helpful advice or criticism that causes our partner to become defensive or withdraw, thereby creating distance in the relationship and confirming our unconscious belief that we don't deserve love. Even if we're loved, we may end up feeling unloved. Narcissists and perfectionists zero in on why their partner is unworthy of love or why they themselves aren't truly receiving the love they want. They devalue their partner's self-esteem and destroy the love that was there. The Accommodators who love them may object, but nonetheless stay, because they, too, unconsciously don't feel worthy of love.

Our Critic can also chip away at our self-esteem, making us feel like a failure if we're single and creating a desperate need to find or stay in a relationship—even a toxic one. This is particularly true of Accommodators, for whom love is the solution to emptiness and shame. They both deny and accept unacceptable behavior due to fear of abandonment and the inability to set boundaries. Despite their resentment, they accept crumbs that offer hope their partner will change.

Autonomy

The word *autonomy* comes from the combination of two Latin words: *auto*, meaning "self," and *nomos*, meaning "law." Together, they mean the ability to govern our own life and actions. When we're autonomous, we're a whole person—an individual, separate from others. Autonomous people enjoy high levels of psychological health and social functioning. They aren't alienated from their real self, and they have an increased sense of well-being and self-esteem. This enables them to make their own choices and take responsibility for their lives.

Autonomy is a feeling of both separateness and wholeness. When we're autonomous, we feel a sense of individuality while in a relationship and a sense of completeness when not, and we have an easier time with relationships and intimacy. We feel comfortable saying no even when we feel pressured because our actions are determined by our internal beliefs, needs, and values. We have a reasonable amount of control over our thoughts and emotions. We're able to compromise and to listen to our partner without reacting emotionally.

It's been said that "You can love only in proportion to your capacity for independence."[5] In healthy relationships, where each person is autonomous, there are fewer demands on one another to be a certain way. Couples still need and depend on each other and are influenced by outside factors, but their behavior reflects personal choice, including sometimes going along with their partner's wishes. Their emotions don't block them from considering new information and their personal needs and wants. These qualities reflect a healthy individuation process—becoming separate individuals developmentally—in each partner, and generally we gravitate toward someone with a similar level of individuation.

Sometimes, a codependent begins recovery, grows, and becomes "counterdependent," maintaining rigid boundaries in reaction to having been dependent for so long. Counterdependence is based on the fear of losing one's autonomy and not true inter-dependence. When someone individuates in a relationship, but his or her partner doesn't, the less individuated partner with lower self-esteem can then start to feel anxious and abandoned because he or she is unable to manipulate the more autonomous partner, who might tire of the drama and not want to be pressured to fulfill those demands.

Because codependents aren't autonomous, they have difficulty tolerating separateness and differences. We're controlled to varying extents by what others do, think, and feel. We emphasize the *we* or the *you* of relationships and lose sight of the *I*. When we love someone, we want to merge in order to complete ourselves. The threat of rejection or of a relationship ending becomes terrifying, and the loss of it agonizing, not only because shame is activated, but also because the other person and the relationship were compensating for deficits we see in ourselves—our perceived lack of wholeness. This is particularly true for Accommodators, who have the greatest need for others, and when they're not in a relationship they heap shame on themselves as proof of how unlovable they are. Some of us remain in a painful, or even abusive, marriage because we'd feel guilty abandoning our spouse or we lack the autonomy that would enable us to leave.

The old adage "opposites attract" is true to the degree that people look to a relationship in order to complete what's missing in their self-development. One person may admire another's creativity, ability to express emotions, boldness, or goal-directedness, because these are traits he or she is lacking. Because Accommodators aren't authoritative, they prefer a subordinate role. They're unlikely to choose another Accommodator as a partner—thinking him or her weak or needy, like themselves—but are in awe of a Master's "strength" and ability to self-direct. They may seek that person's protection and bask in the reflection of his or her success, power, and charisma. By living vicariously through a Master, they don't develop their own assertiveness or power.

Similarly, Accommodators are typically drawn to those who appear bold and express anger because their own is repressed, often shame-bound, and frightening to them. Initially, they feel protected by the Master's ability to take charge or stand up to others. Accommodators don't realize that Masters often have a fragile persona, are easily deflated, and actually feel ashamed and insecure inside. Masters don't want to be with someone who is too independent or who will challenge them and make them feel weak. They're attracted to Accommodators whom they can control and who support their pride and fill their emptiness when they're alone. They may be drawn to Accommodators who are emotionally expressive and nurturing, qualities they themselves lack.

Bystanders, those who shy away from relationships to avoid conflict and to preserve their freedom, also lack autonomy, but put up walls in order to protect their fragile sense of self from others' expectations or pressure. They have trouble separating their own desires from those of others and withdraw rather than being influenced. In a relationship, they try to satisfy their need for freedom by not getting emotionally close to anyone. An Accommodator would feel frustrated and continually abandoned in a relationship with a Bystander, who would pull away from pressure for intimacy. Bystanders are comfortable in a relationship with someone who has similar needs for distance. The two would want a marriage with little closeness and with ample time apart—even maintaining separate bedrooms or abodes. This sort of isolation is not the same as emotional autonomy, which permits closeness, although their lifestyle may look that way to outsiders.

Autonomy has a big impact on how well we get along with others and on intimate relationships. Relationships based on compensating for lack of wholeness and individual inadequacy don't endure as well as relationships where both partners are more autonomous.[6] When we develop our real self and become an individual *I*, our relationships can better tolerate differences and separateness. As partners, we make our relationship a priority but are autonomous enough to meet many of our own needs and feel content when we're alone. We enjoy the parts of our life outside the relationship and don't feel abandoned by our partner's need for separateness. Although we may be lonely at times, we realize that being in a relationship is a preference and not something we require in order to feel okay about ourselves and our life. We know that we can survive alone and that endings, although painful, need not be devastating. In fact, autonomy and self-acceptance lead to the discovery that we don't need to find true love in order to have a fulfilled life.[7]

Individuation also enables us to think about and perceive the world and other people clearly in the here and now, not filtered through beliefs, rules, or needs originating in the past.

Idealization

Lack of wholeness and shame work together to fuel what's known as *idealization*, or imbuing a partner with traits that we desire or have disowned in ourselves, hoping to absorb those qualities from him or her. For example, we may not acknowledge our own creativity, power, kindness, spirituality, or intelligence but only see it reflected back to us in someone else.

Generally, this is an unconscious process. When we idealize, we're coming from a place of feeling "less than." We raise others up and lower ourselves in comparison. The more we idealize another person, the more power that person holds over us.

The maxim "Love is blind" refers to limerence, or the romantic falling-in-love stage when two people—even people with healthy relationship skills—idealize each other. When codependents attach to someone they admire and idealize, the unconscious thought is, *If someone this wonderful accepts me, I must not be so bad.* This is a big motivation for falling in love. In fact, during dating, couples bond and feel closer by sharing their frailties and inadequacies, which is also a way to test if their despicable self is acceptable.[8] Masters and Accommodators may try to rescue someone they idealize and who needs them, such as an addict, to buoy their sense of importance and self-worth.

Figure 6.1

The Paradox of Shame

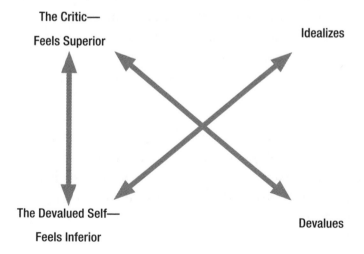

Figure 6.1 illustrates the many faces of shame. The divided self is made up of the superior-acting, shaming Critic and the inferior, devalued self. When the devalued self is in the inferior position, shame manifests by idealizing others. When shame is defended, and it's in a superior position, it devalues others. Most codependents fluctuate between the inferior or superior positions, but some are predominantly one or the other, such as a narcissist or a person whose personality is dominated by shame. Both devaluation and idealization are commensurate with the severity of shame and the associated depression.

As part of healthy psychological development, children idealize their parents in order to internalize their characteristics and functions. Normally, as we mature we grow to see our parents in a more realistic light. For codependents, this may require working through the shame, grief, and anger connected to painful experiences and messages from childhood, so that parents are no longer seen as weak or powerful figures but are accepted as separate, though flawed, individuals. They become human beings, not idealized or fallen heroes.

If the natural process of de-idealization of a parent happens prematurely, or is interrupted due to a trauma (such as physical, sexual, or emotional abuse or a parent's early death), a child doesn't experience a healthy incorporation of parental values, ideals, and functions. As adults, we will hunger for and seek out those missing parts of the self in romantic partners whom we idealize and depend on.[9] Hence, in choosing a mate, women and men frequently sexualize and idealize partners who unconsciously remind them of their fathers and mothers, respectively. They unwittingly project and idealize characteristics of their parent(s), a sibling, or other loved one to make up for their missing traits, rather than clearly seeing a romantic prospect as a unique individual not idealized—with both positive and negative traits.

Cynthia came to see me because she was unhappy in her romance with a selfish narcissist, with whom she was obsessed. Then it struck her that the man's physical features were just like those of her late, adoring father. As she began to fully grieve the loss of her father, her infatuation instantly vanished. In another case, Jonathan was married to Teresa, a large, seductive, but distant woman, reminiscent of his adoring but unavailable mother. Although he was unhappy, he couldn't end the relationship. Cynthia and Jonathan didn't really love their partners but became attached because they needed to develop the internal functions they didn't develop in childhood. In partnering with their "fathers" and "mothers," couples are driven by the unconscious need to heal those primary relationships. Their spouse would initially be seen as a "good father" or "good mother." In magically restoring their longed-for parent, they're seeking to heal shame and childhood wounds that get stirred up by intense emotions in their present relationship.[10]

In actuality, love isn't based on idealization but on real knowledge and acceptance of each other gained through familiarity over time. Healthy couples reinforce each other's self-esteem, and they may idealize to a minor extent, but not in order to fill each other's emptiness or deny their own negative feelings. Compare the progression of love in codependent and healthy relationships in Table 6.2.

When idealization produces major distortions, there's bound to be disappointment as the romance wears off. The shortcomings we at first overlooked surface and shatter our idealized image, and we're often dissatisfied with the truth of who our partner is. We discover that he or she has the same negative qualities as our parent(s). We become critical, contemptuous,

Table 6.2. **Progression of Love**

Codependent Relationships	Healthy Relationships
Intense attraction—feel anxious	Friendship begins—feel comfortable
Idealize each other and ignore differences	Get to know each other
Fall in love and make commitments	Acknowledge differences (or leave)
Get to know each other	Grow to love each other
Become disappointed	Make commitments
Cling to romantic fantasy of love	Negotiate and compromise needs
Try to change partner into ideal	Love and acceptance of each other deepens
Feel resentful and unloved	Feel supported and loved

and disapproving,[11] and try to change our partner into our idealized image. Masters and Accommodators develop disdain for each other. Now the idealization fueled by shame switches to devaluation. Accommodators discover that their partner's boldness or protection is now anger and control directed toward them (sometimes in reaction to their own passive-aggressive behavior). They feel unloved, disrespected, and victimized yet can't set boundaries. Masters are repelled by what they perceive to be an Accommodator's weakness and emotional neediness.

Separateness versus Closeness

As human beings, one of our deepest primal needs is to overcome separateness. Yet we all have dual needs for separateness and closeness as well as for independence and dependency. Most relationship problems revolve around the negotiation of needs for physical and emotional separateness and closeness. Separateness can include time alone, career goals, personal hobbies, individual friends, creativity, and spirituality. As codependents, we sometimes confuse which needs we should meet on our own (autonomy) and which needs we can depend on others to meet (dependency). Some of us are extreme, either wanting someone else to meet all our emotional needs or believing we must be emotionally self-sufficient.

Relationships are further complicated when fears are stimulated about abandonment or losing autonomy and independence. Frequently, these fears are unconscious. We might develop anxiety around getting hurt or feeling insecure or trapped. The bottom line is, "Will I get enough love or be abandoned?" or "Will I lose my independence or be smothered?" These fears, along with shame, make us fear intimacy. Shame provokes anxiety about self-disclosure and becoming dependent on someone who might reject, control, hurt, or abandon us. Yet we're conflicted because, on the other hand, we also feel lonely and empty, and yearn to find a partner to provide the love we missed growing up. The vulnerabilities of childhood—being dependent on a parent whose love was inadequate—get replayed in intimate relationships.

Figure 6.2

Continuum of Intimacy

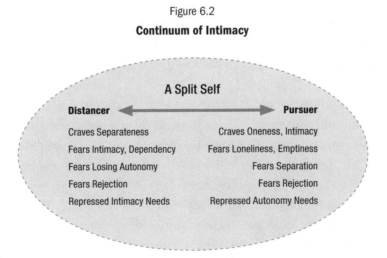

A Split Self

Distancer ⟷ Pursuer

Distancer	Pursuer
Craves Separateness	Craves Oneness, Intimacy
Fears Intimacy, Dependency	Fears Loneliness, Emptiness
Fears Losing Autonomy	Fears Separation
Fears Rejection	Fears Rejection
Repressed Intimacy Needs	Repressed Autonomy Needs

Depending on our personality and with whom we might be getting involved, we may adopt one of two behavior patterns and become either the pursuer or the distancer. Both the *fear of abandonment and need for intimacy felt by a pursuer and the fear of intimacy and the need for distance felt by a distancer,* as listed in Figure 6.2, are more or less unconscious. A pursuer who was hurt in one relationship might become a distancer in the next. These designations are artificial stereotypes for the purpose of discussing behavior and underlying motives. Most people fluctuate on a continuum. However, when they're in one role, they're usually only conscious of their need for intimacy or distance and are unconscious of the opposite need, which they witness in their romantic partner. They're attracted to the other in order to become whole.

Pursuers are unconscious of their fear of intimacy and their autonomy needs, often thought of as separate activities, time, and space. They rely on distancers to create space in order to experience independence and avoid intimacy, and so they pursue unavailable distancers. Distancers are unconscious of their fear of abandonment and their need for intimacy. They don't experience the need for closeness as their own and rely on pursuers to open them to their emotions, intimacy, and dependency needs. It could be said that "Inside every distancer is a pursuer, and inside every pursuer is a distancer."[12] However, these roles ebb and flow within relationships and diminish when partners individuate and become more whole. But some people can tolerate neither closeness nor being alone. Both provoke too much anxiety.

Pursuers

For pursuers, being alone is too painful. It stimulates feelings of emptiness, loneliness, and unlovability, reminiscent of the abandonment they experienced in childhood. Some pursuers desperately forfeit "anything for love." In order to bolster their deficient self, they long to *merge* with their partner to fulfill their ideal relationship where *we* become *one*. Accommodators in particular seek relationships to fulfill their need for love and validation. Love makes them feel lovable and worthy and offers the promise of healing past wounds with newfound happiness through a life partner. Love presents the answer to their emptiness and loneliness and a means to fulfill many unmet needs. Rather than use their own efforts to effectively respond to their innate drive toward wholeness, they crave love to heal the divide between their Critic and real self, and they want to love as much as be loved to perfect their devoted, idealized self.[13] Masters are also pursuers, but are motivated by power and the need for admiration. They can be very charming and sexually seductive but retreat as the relationship progresses and as their partner, usually an Accommodator, desires more intimacy.

Because of their shame, pursuers hide who they really are when dating, sometimes behind seduction, to lure a mate. Sexual attraction becomes the basis for fantasies about the relationship and the other person. The pursuer's imagination fills with idealized details about the object of his or her attention. To allay their fears, pursuers quickly think *we* are in a relationship and want to be a "couple," sometimes overlooking the distancer's slower pace or even retreat. They dissect communications, looking for hopeful signs, and analyze the distancer's personality, focusing on and idealizing positive traits and similarities while overlooking any potential problems and even facts to the contrary. They may idealize partners who reject them or who are unavailable because, due to low self-esteem, they unconsciously believe they have to earn love. (See Figure 6.1.) It brings to mind the Groucho Marx joke, "I don't care to belong to any club that will have *me* as a member."

Pursuers wait for phone calls and plan their activities around the distancer's availability, ignoring their friends and their own interests, even feigning delight in those of their partner. They easily feel insecure and dejected when their partner wants to do something independently or with other friends. Initially, pursuers are afraid to ask for their needs to be met because they fear abandonment. They do everything possible to please the distancer and meet his or her needs instead, to make the relationship work. Intermittently, real or perceived rejection ushers in the shame of being unacceptable, along with fears and despair about the relationship failing or never finding a mate. Pursuers then defend against these feelings with hope and denial and by further attempting to accommodate the distancer. In a sense, the distancer's rejection breaks the pursuer's pride and defenses, enabling the pursuer to surrender to love,[14] for pursuers find it impossible to love someone who pursues them.

When the chase is over and the couple gets to know one another better (which can take years, depending on the degree of idealization and denial), they often experience the differences they initially disregarded. Even after commitments are made, the pattern continues. In time, pursuers become resentful that they're always accommodating the distancer's schedule and attempt to control and change him or her to be less "selfish," spend more time together, and be more attentive. The pursuer complains of not receiving more affection, assurances of love, or communication about the relationship, and wants the distancer to be more involved with the pursuer's activities, friends, and family. The pursuer concludes that his or her partner is inconsiderate, self-centered, and inflexible.

In reality, pursuers have disowned their shame-bound need for separateness, which is both projected onto and embodied in their distancing mate. Still, they may cling to the relationship because they're afraid of ending up alone. Intense initial attraction followed by suffering or conflict frequently indicates that the relationship was motivated by attempts to avoid shame and emptiness and is an addictive attachment.[15]

Distancers

Distancers are more aware than pursuers of their fear of closeness but are unconscious of their need for intimacy. They've chosen an illusion of self-sufficiency and believe that they don't need anyone. Being close exposes them to the shame of feeling needy and dependent, especially if their needs were shamed or not met in their childhood. For the distancer, the thought of becoming dependent can be just as terrifying as the pursuer's fear of being abandoned.

Distancers maintain boundaries so they will not feel devoured or smothered by the pursuer's needs or attention. They also push away potential partners because they feel unworthy of love and fear being found deficient. To protect themselves, they avoid feelings and intimacy, thereby precluding potential rejection, vulnerability, and shame. Still, they're drawn to the excitement, emotionality, and risk-taking of the pursuer, who can vitalize their emotionless persona.

Whereas pursuers quickly want to be a couple and share everything together, distancers cautiously protect their time, space, and belongings. They want a relationship, but only if it's on their terms and at their slow pace, passively allowing the pursuer to give, accommodate, and energize the relationship. They emphasize *I*, practicalities, and perceived differences. Their unilateral decisions about the relationship hurt the pursuer, who feels unimportant and uncared for. Distancers only experience their need for closeness when there's enough space for them to feel their inner emptiness or if their partner threatens to leave.

Although Accommodators may be distancers, Bystanders and Masters more commonly play this role once they sense that more than sex is anticipated and being vulnerable and emotionally close threatens their power and control. The thought of being dependent is abhorrent to them. It not only limits their options and makes them feel weak, but it also exposes them to rejection and feeling shame, which they avoid at all costs.

Addicts commonly use their addiction to create distance and avoid the perils of intimacy. Some distancers have a romance addiction to a fantasy or online relationship that they can control. Their mind is filled with scenarios and daydreams to avoid experiencing their loneliness and intimacy needs that would motivate them to seek a real relationship.

For example, Jane was abandoned by her father when she was six. She internalized a message of her unlovability and unconsciously concluded that she couldn't trust men and would have to rely solely on herself. She chose men who reinforced her beliefs and the necessity to be alone and self-sufficient. Nevertheless, her shame, her longing for a partner, and her pain about the inability to find someone were real. She turned to self-soothing addictive relationships with alcohol and food, which she could control, at least for a while. Jane's cycle of abandonment is depicted in Figure 6.3.

Addicts also use their addiction as a defense to avoid feelings and intimacy. In effect, they're saying, "I don't need you. I can feed and take care of myself."[16] Distance allows them to feel intact without being engulfed by someone else and to withdraw rather than share feelings or talk out problems. The other dynamic that can be at play for addicts is their need to protect their obsessive relationship with their drug of choice,

Figure 6.3

Cycle of Abandonment

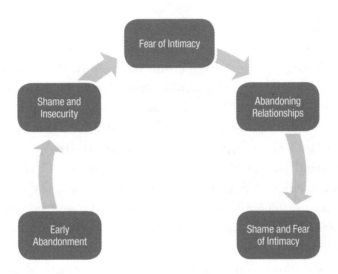

which intimacy or the demands of other relationships can threaten.

Perfectionist distancers can have a compulsive need to find fault in potential partners. They cling to the idea that eventually they'll meet the "perfect" person. At times, distancers doubt whether they're capable of love. They need the pursuer's admiration to confirm their idealized self and to compensate for their shame. Their rigid boundaries protect their incomplete self from feeling invaded or smothered, which is intensified if they grew up with a controlling or invasive parent.

Distancers feel troubled by the smothering demands of their pursuer, who appears needy and dependent—traits they despise in themselves. The pursuer's expectations trigger their shame and guilt, causing them to feel unappreciated, criticized, and that what they give isn't enough to satisfy the pursuer. More demands for togetherness only breed contempt and push the distancer further away. Their retreat escalates the pursuer's fears of abandonment, which make the pursuer behave and appear even needier, thus perpetuating the couple's negative cycle.

To avoid intimacy, some couples may have long-distance relationships. They may argue at the end of their periodic reunions in anticipation of a painful separation. When they're apart, their images of each other may alternate between romantic fantasies and worry and judgment and resentment. Pursuers miss the distancer and daydream to fill their emptiness and deny feelings of loneliness and rejection. Distancers feel relief from the anxiety of being engulfed by the pursuer's needs, from becoming dependent, and from the possibility of being abandoned due to their own inadequacy. The nature of their relationship avoids intimacy for both partners who feel unlovable, but blame one another.

Ending Polarization

As we get further from our partner, polarization can occur. We each take an opposite corner in the boxing ring, and any little thing can trigger one of us to start throwing punches in the form of either an argument or withdrawal. We create power struggles about anything under the sun—family, finances, chores, children, or any significant decision. But if we look deeper, our real worry is either about giving up independence or whether we're secure and loved enough. Men may worry more about the former and women the latter, but not necessarily, and they may switch roles. Some relationships become stuck in a power struggle of mutual dissatisfaction. Partners blame each other for their problems.

To break the polarization, we need to avoid distancing when we feel smothered and avoid pursuing when we feel abandoned.

Change takes tremendous strength and courage and requires us to be aware of our fears and the defenses we use to avoid closeness, shame, and emptiness. When pursuers refrain from making demands and tire of pursuing, and distancers stop defending and running, they each experience their fears and emptiness.[17] When we finally stop and face these uncomfortable feelings, we can accept them for what they are. This acceptance reduces our anxiety and helps us redirect our energy toward becoming whole. Eventually, we'll know that if the relationship doesn't work out, we'll be fine.

Carmela never felt truly loved by her narcissistic father. Her feelings of unlovability created a desperate need to be loved by a man. She either pushed away available suitors or pursued those who weren't, and then returned to feeling lonely and unlovable, as she always had. Her pursuits were failed attempts to escape the grief and loneliness of her childhood, but she kept re-creating the scenario despite her efforts to avoid it. Carmela found her way out by grieving and coming to terms with her past, facing her feelings of hopelessness and emptiness, and learning to love herself.

Nothing comes from pursuing a distancer. Pursuers must stop what they've been doing and tolerate the anxiety of separation and of saying no. They need to acknowledge their own emptiness, as painful as it may be. The feelings of shame about being alone and unlovable from childhood can then surface and be healed. As pursuers reconnect with their real self, they learn to take responsibility for their needs and create fulfillment and meaning in their life. They can learn to be more autonomous and independent by emulating the distancer.

If you're a pursuer, look at how you manipulate others to create closeness and ensure you won't be abandoned. Are you seductive, controlling, pleasing, caretaking? Do you disown your autonomy by accommodating the distancer, giving up outside friends and interests? Do you avoid disagreeing or saying no, even when you'd like to? What is your motive for doing this, and how does it affect you? Although you hate being ignored, do you ignore your own needs?

Distancers need to develop awareness of their feelings and defenses. This helps them identify and explore their anxiety. Instead of resisting an internal feeling of obligation toward their partner, they can set boundaries and discern whether they actually want to be close. By resisting the urge to automatically pull away, they realize that their behavior is covering up their shame and their terror of being smothered, controlled, or rejected. Healing requires them to understand and explore their fears and childhood wounds. It also entails distancers accepting that they're enough just as they are. They gain compassion for their needs and stop judging themselves for being needy, dependent, and vulnerable. Distancers discover that it's safe to talk about real feelings and that it's okay to risk saying, "I miss you. I need you."

If you're a distancer, notice when you want to be close—not out of obligation but out of a desire for closeness. Observe when, how, and why you withdraw. What does it remind you of? What happened to make you shut down emotionally? When did you decide that self-sufficiency is safer than love? What did you sacrifice in this bargain?

As couples build their self-esteem and become conscious of their individual needs for both closeness and separateness, they take responsibility for their own needs and can respect the needs of their partner. They feel more worthy of love and are able to receive it without ignoring, discounting, or rejecting it, so neither of them is polarized into being a pursuer or a distancer. They no longer bother pursuing an unavailable person who can't or doesn't love them; both the pursuer and the distancer can now appreciate someone who does. Distancers are able to say yes without fear of being smothered by closeness, and pursuers can say no without fear of rejection or separation. Each can ask for togetherness and space directly—without manipulation, guilt, or blame. Something so simple actually requires a healthy amount of self-esteem, assertiveness, and courage. As couples work on this process, they have more authentic intimacy, rather than becoming locked into an unconscious duet of approach and avoidance.[18] They gain greater empathy for one another, are more able to listen to each other's needs, and compromise with greater understanding.

Communication and Conflict

Codependents often imagine that relationships alone can solve their emptiness and loneliness without them having to open up and expose their real self. Their shame anxiety and associated defenses become the enemy of the love they seek. When they feel hurt or vulnerable—which is an opportunity that healthy couples use to open up and create genuine intimacy— codependents generally avoid connecting through honest communication. Instead, they react by either withdrawing or attacking. Anger can escalate into destructive cycles of hot or cold wars. The greater the shame and insecurity, the more dysfunctional the communication becomes.

Become Assertive

How we communicate reflects our level of self-esteem. We might not realize we're being dishonest in relationships or that we're withholding or distorting information to reveal only what we want in order to protect ourselves from others' disapproval. We have trouble being direct and are careful to never take a position or reveal our true self, lest others disagree and not like us. Most of us claim that we hide the truth to avoid hurting someone else's feelings, but underneath we fear disapproval or a rupture in the relationship. Such deception and people-pleasing are methods of "covert manipulation" that codependents commonly use to control conversation and behavior, which undermines trust and closeness in relationships.

In reality, we'd rather protect ourselves than get close, and in the end we'd rather trade true security and fulfillment for a false sense of safety. Eventually, couples build barriers and behave in predictable, deadening patterns, including blame, compliance, and even romantic scripts that substitute for a vibrant connection. But by risking authentic, assertive communication, we open the door to passion, intimacy, and love. Understanding and empathy are essential to having a genuine connection and to giving and receiving love.

Healthy, honest, assertive communication creates intimacy— the stuff real relationships are made of. To be assertive, we express feelings with "I" statements. Assertiveness is a behavior we can learn, and it can significantly raise self-esteem, which is something I wrote about in *How to Speak Your Mind: Become Assertive and Set Limits.* Saying yes to avoid saying no or evading discussion about problems leads to resentment, conflict, diminished intimacy, and deterioration of the relationship. When we're direct about our feelings and not afraid to say no, we give others permission to do so as well. It also makes asking for needs and wants less terrifying.

For codependents, being assertive is complicated by the fact that we're largely unaware of our feelings and needs. We're used to reacting or expressing judgments. Instead of saying, "*I'm* hurt (or disappointed)," we say, "*You* only think about yourself" or "*You* always _____." Rather than ask for what we want or need, we continue to argue and criticize with statements such as "*You* never _____."

Using "I" statements helps us name our needs. But first we must be able to identify our needs and feel worthy of having them met. If our needs are shame-bound, we may not know that we're missing tenderness or affection or expect cooperation and to be treated with courtesy. As a child, I wished my mother would bake cookies, not knowing that what I really missed was nurturing. Then, in my twenties, I missed taking walks with my husband. I didn't have words for what I really was missing: connection and intimacy.

Avoid Expecting Others to Mind-Read

If we do know what we want or need, we risk humiliation by asking for it. Instead, we expect our partner to know how his or her behavior makes us feel and to "read our mind." When this doesn't happen, we're disappointed and complain. We might feel unimportant and unloved, which triggers our shame. Our "mind-reading" assumption is a rationalization to hide our shame about directly making a request. It also presumes that our partner isn't a separate person, but a wished-for extension of our mind—like the all-providing parent we may not have had. The feeling that it doesn't count if we have to ask puts our partner in a double bind—damned if they do fulfill a request and damned if they don't—all of which creates conflict.

A variation of this is when we presume to know what our partner is thinking or feeling. When we analyze, label, tell someone what they feel, or say, "Your problem is . . . ," we ignore mental and emotional boundaries. The implication is that one person is superior and all-knowing. Such statements are felt as intrusive attacks, patronizing, and shaming. It's more respectful if we ask about our partner's feelings with an open mind.

Understand and Respect Boundaries

Boundaries are those invisible lines we use to separate ourselves from others. Boundaries are how we set limits internally and externally. We may, for instance, accept that our husband swears on occasion because he's upset, but we might have zero tolerance for listening to a rampage. That's a boundary that we set based on what we feel is acceptable behavior.

Healthy relationships require that partners set healthy limits to prevent resentment and abuse. But because we can have difficulty setting boundaries, we experience others' boundaries as a shaming statement about us. We might view the time a partner spends on individual hobbies or friends as selfishness. Our wife's desire for separateness becomes proof that we're not worth spending time with. Healthy relationships demand time together and time alone. Just about any type of withdrawal can trigger feelings of shame. When we react to our partner's boundaries this way, we're confusing actions with feelings and personalizing our partner's needs. When we learn to set boundaries and to accept our partner's boundaries, our relationship can improve by leaps and bounds.

Resist the Urge to Caretake and Control

Our attempts to improve our partner breed conflict and resentment, and may result in enabling the very behavior we want to discourage. To illustrate how this works, we'll use the example of the Top Dog and the Under Dog. The helper Top Dog in Figure 6.4 feels self-sufficient and superior, while the Under Dog feels ineffective and inferior, creating an unbalanced relationship. The Top Dog shames the Under Dog by helping or finding flaws to improve, invading the Under Dog's boundaries. (See Figure 6.4.) At their core, both feel inadequate and unworthy. Perfectionist Top Dogs deflect their

Figure 6.4

Top Dog and Under Dog Caretaking

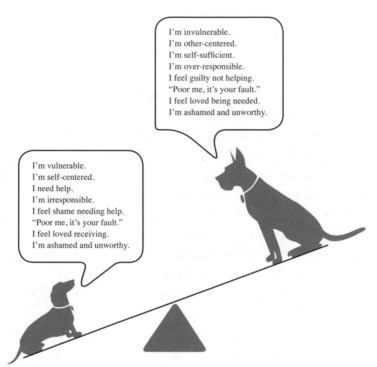

shame when they nit-pick, making life intolerable for their partner.

Partners may play different roles in different arenas. For example, a wife might be the Top Dog in parenting, while her husband is the Top Dog when it comes to their finances. But they can also quickly switch positions. These roles can automatically trigger childhood shaming patterns with Top Dog playing the critical parent and Under Dog playing the devalued child. When the Under Dog plays the victim, it prompts the Top Dog to offer advice, criticism, or help, which sometimes is met with the Under Dog's verbal abuse. Now, the Top Dog is the victim.

My client Candace regularly sought her husband Ted's help with their kids, but consistently complained and discounted his attempts to help until he'd ultimately become frustrated and irritable, at which point she became angry and accusatory. This is a version of the "Yes, but–Kick me" dynamic, where the "victim" spouse (Candace) provokes the "helper" (Ted) into meeting her need to be persecuted (kicked), and then she proceeds to persecute and victimize him.

A couple's pattern may be occasional or ongoing and carry with it the potential to create distance and an imbalance in the relationship, particularly when abuse is involved. We can get stuck in our roles for years, making life miserable for both parties. In order to change, Top Dogs must resist advising and controlling, lower their expectations of the Under Dog, refocus back on their real self, and problem-solve from a "we" perspective. Without anyone to make the Under Dog feel better, both partners are forced to disengage, deal with their inner emptiness and pain, and become self-responsible. This brings the relationship back into balance. The partners may not be happy about the situation initially, but eventually they can begin to grapple with reality, learn to accept one another, or possibly end the relationship.

What responsibilities of your own do you neglect? Do you assume responsibilities that are actually your partner's? Are you making assumptions, or have the two of you had a frank discussion and negotiated shared responsibilities? How could you express your needs and feelings assertively? How would you feel if your partner never changed? Can you accept that possibility?

Avoid Escalating Conflict

If we're hypersensitive to criticism and shame, we may take words and behaviors personally, whether or not they were intended as criticism. Because of our shame and poor boundaries, we might wrongly interpret our partner's moods and emotions as a negative statement about us. Women more than men easily tend to make global self-attributions of shame based on their partner's gestures or loud or passionate tones that weren't intended to be derogatory.[19] Women are also more sensitive to anger, but both men and women can easily misinterpret requests as orders and suggestions as criticism.

When we misperceive and then defend, attack with anger and blame, or refuse to continue a discussion, we create an emotional rift. Reactive behavior triggers a shame response in our partner, which can escalate conflict, and before we know it we're in a destructive cycle, where we both are defending feelings of rejection and unlovability. Invariably, couples disagree about what happened or what was actually said. Although the Critic can distort perception, there's usually at least a kernel of truth to each partner's story. To know what really happened, we have to closely examine our inner and outer dialogues, but this is hard to do after a heated argument. Most couples need an objective listener such as a counselor.

A typical pattern is when a husband wants to please his wife, but feels inadequate and unappreciated when he senses her discontent with his efforts. Many women are sensitive and self-critical about their appearance. Therefore, the wife could easily interpret her husband's lack of compliments, particularly when she is dressed up, as indication of his disapproval and disappointment. Arguments often occur when the husband doesn't respond to his wife's requests for help with chores, child care, or repairs. He might feel micromanaged by her when he does help. In her mind, she's merely trying to explain what she needs, but he's feeling controlled, diminished, and shamed and may react by withdrawing.

Another scenario is when husbands make decisions without consulting their wives. Women often interpret this as meaning their needs and opinions don't matter. Some husbands question their wife's expenditures because they worry, feel insecure as a breadwinner (despite a substantial income), or assume their work efforts are unappreciated. She, on the other hand, feels scolded, blamed, and controlled, and arguments ensue. He's too ashamed to admit his worries and too fearful to relinquish control and take a "we" problem-solving approach, which would change the direction of the conversation. (If a spouse has a gambling or spending addiction, for example, setting boundaries would be appropriate.)

People who feel humiliated often criticize their partner for specific behaviors, such as drunkenness in public. Rather than share their embarrassment and shame, or appropriately deal with an addicted partner, they transfer their shame by blaming. The scolded partner, especially if he or she is an alcoholic, defends with denial or returns shaming attacks to avoid looking at his or her own behavior.

Accommodators hate conflict. They have difficulty accessing their power and anger and stating what they don't like and don't want. Many build up resentment and express their anger through judgment and control or withdrawal. Instead of setting boundaries or talking things over, Accommodators, as well as Bystanders, may behave in a passive-aggressive manner by withholding emotionally or sexually or by being uncooperative, late, detached, or disagreeable. When either partner withdraws or avoids sex or emotional intimacy, the other feels rejected and unimportant. Accommodators, as well as Bystanders, may agree to do something they'd rather not but then become detached or disagreeable.

These are only a few of the limitless examples of conflicts that produce irresolvable, escalating power struggles and reciprocal shaming in intimate relationships. Regardless of the partners' motivations, once they feel criticized or abandoned, or are made to feel less than, they initiate defenses to internalized shame in order to feel safe or more powerful. Because of shame, they also have difficulty accepting responsibility for their actions or accepting any feedback. Instead, they use defensive excuses and denials that escalate arguments. Worse, they shift responsibility by blaming and projecting guilt and shame onto their partner, who then becomes defensive as well.

On the surface these conflicts might seem impossible to resolve, but they're really just red herrings. The real conflict is inside us. By healing shame and low self-esteem, we're able to take responsibility for our behavior. We become more assertive and develop healthier boundaries, which enables us to risk disapproval by being direct and honest. There's more freedom, space, and respect in the relationship, making it safer to share feelings, ask for needs, and say no. Instead of reacting, we respond assertively. When we express our limitations and hurt feelings, we can see each other as separate and vulnerable, lower our defenses and expectations, and empathize. We learn to express our needs, disagree, compromise, and accept one another. We build bridges to establish mutual understanding and closeness through shared vulnerability. In the future, conflicts are less likely to escalate into irresolvable arguments.

Abusive Relationships

If someone talks to us in a shaming way, we're most likely being verbally abused. Verbal abuse exists in many codependent relationships. Name-calling, ordering, or raging are obvious examples, but criticizing, blaming, threatening, belittling, and interrogating are also abusive and hurtful. Even analyzing or lecturing can be felt as shaming to the listener. Other subtle forms of abuse include cruel teasing, manipulation, withholding, sarcasm, and interrupting.

Sometimes the abuse does not involve verbal or physical attacks, but rather withholding—of warmth and affection, communication, sex, or material things. Abusers are attempting to fortify themselves against their own internalized shame by transferring it to others, and in the process ignore others' boundaries. To stop the abuse, victims need to establish those boundaries.

Self-effacing Accommodators, uncomfortable with their own aggression, are drawn to Masters, including selfish narcissists, volatile people who have borderline personalities, addicts, and abusers who behave aggressively. Needing to feel superior, abusers transfer their internal shame to compensate for feeling weak and inferior. (See Figure 6.1.) Accommodators sacrifice themselves and tolerate abuse because of their own lack of self-worth. They may be in denial of the abuse that others see. Some pine away, longing for affection and signs of love, similar to Echo in the myth of Narcissus, who died waiting for the acknowledgment she never received.

Although others may recognize that the abuser is a weak bully, an abuser is powerful and intimidating to the Accommodator, who becomes helpless in the face of abuse. Abusers may be emulating an abusive parent, and their victims respond just as they did in childhood when they lacked protection. When attacked or criticized, Accommodators are defensive and apologetic, and placate and appease to calm the abuser. But by placating rather than confronting abusive behavior, they invite more aggression and blame. Even those who fight back are unable to set firm boundaries. What's more, Accommodators fear emotional abandonment even worse than abuse, because maintaining the relationship is their priority. The more they fear abandonment and anger, the more they walk on eggshells to accommodate the abuser.

Some Accommodators unconsciously desire someone to humiliate them just as their inner Critic does—a mate who sees the worst in them but still "loves" them. The rationale is "Only my tormentor has seen and punished me for my badness, yet still loves me." The victim is cleansed, and, temporarily, the fear of torment is banished.[20] These relationships are often passionate. An abuser may have a Jekyll-and-Hyde personality, often induced by drugs or alcohol. Mr. Hyde tears down, and Dr. Jekyll builds up with love, hooking and giving hope to the partner.

Accommodators may martyr themselves "for love" and continue to be mistreated by a partner for years. To support their denial, they rationalize their suffering by trying to be compassionate, while feeling morally superior. In her work, Karen Horney found that self-effacing Accommodators often feel they need their pride broken by someone more powerful in order to surrender and love.[21] After being debased, in exchange for their sacrifice, pride and a sense of moral superiority eventually resurface and provide a defense to internalized shame. Humiliated as children, Accommodators unconsciously exact revenge for the sins of their parents out of hatred, not love.[22]

Typically, abusers take no responsibility and blame their victim for their actions. Nevertheless, both parties feel shamed by the abuse. Abusers feel shame for losing control. Victims feel shame because they feel unworthy, because shame has been transferred to them by the abuser, and because they believe the abuser's accusations. Abusive relationships perpetuate shame and encourage secrecy due to the stigma associated with abuse and violence. Neither partner is inclined to confide in others or reach out for help, particularly in the early stages. But the longer the abuse is permitted, the more it erodes the victim's self-esteem.

If you're in an abusive relationship, you need to get professional help. If your partner won't cooperate in getting counseling, you should go on your own and get help in deciding if you need to leave the relationship, especially if there are children involved. If there is physical abuse, report it immediately to the police and engage their help in finding a safe place for you (and your children if you have them) to go, either staying with a friend or relative or going to a safe house in your community. If necessary, you may need to obtain a restraining order if your partner won't take responsibility for his or her actions and get help.

Real Intimacy

Intimate relationships demand courage because they inevitably involve feelings of loss, abandonment, and disappointment. Codependents are easily hurt, and they hurt because love unmasks shame and exposes all their vulnerabilities. Long-term studies confirm that partners will spend years fearing loneliness, vulnerability, rejection, and loss, but—because intimacy is so laden with anxiety—they nevertheless avoid affection and tenderness, despite their silent dreams of idealized love.[23] Donald Nathanson, author of *Shame and Pride: Affect, Sex, and the Birth of the Self,* writes:

Shame haunts our every dream of love. The more we wish for communion, so much more are we vulnerable to the painful augmentation of any impediment, however real or fancied. To love grandly is to risk grand pain. Intimacy with the other validates the value of the self, and any impediment to intimacy causes severe injury to self-experience.[24]

Intimacy requires two kinds of courage: first, the courage to be an individual; and second, courage by both partners to share their true self. Each move they make toward authenticity and intimacy risks exposure, criticism, and rejection of their real self, and annihilation of their ideal self. But facing those risks also affirms their real self. In order to guard this level of vulnerability and create an environment where it's safe to share authentic needs and feelings, trust is vital. Here are the ingredients to real intimacy:[25]

1. Safety

2. Trust

3. Self-awareness

4. Presence

5. Openness and Honesty

6. Courage

7. Self-esteem

8. Autonomy–Separateness

9. Mutuality

Self-awareness, openness, and honesty are derived from self-esteem and connection to the real self. As our real self individuates in recovery, we develop an identity with healthy boundaries.

In relationships, we don't attempt to merge with someone else to become whole. Instead of seeking oneness, we seek *closeness,* because we see our partner as unique and separate. Rather than "loving" an ideal or someone like ourselves, we acknowledge, respect, and appreciate each other's differences. Paradoxically, this greater autonomy allows us to have more capacity for intimacy. We feel comfortable being either separate or close because we can tolerate being alone as well as "opening up" to our partner. With more separateness and self-esteem, we're able to accept our shortcomings, while honoring and taking responsibility for our own needs and feelings, including our emptiness. We can ask directly for what we need from others because we don't feel guilty or ashamed nor responsible for their feelings and needs.

With good self-esteem and autonomy, we can accept—not try to change—our feelings, needs, and limitations, as well as those of our partner. This acceptance is essential for relationships to work. Partners can agree to disagree, have different interests, and spend time alone or with individual friends without triggering feelings of abandonment in their mate. There isn't a need to control. We don't expect each other to change or to feel or act differently. There's an "awareness of complementarity" and an acknowledgment that our mutual differences enrich one another, making real love possible.[26]

The step 6 exercises in chapter 8 relate to sharing our shame with others. If your relationship isn't a safe place to share, or you're not in a relationship, consider finding a safe outlet for talking about your feelings, needs, and limitations, such as a Twelve Step meeting.

The step 7 exercises in chapter 8 will help you develop your autonomy by building up your self-esteem with positive affirmations and actions.

Exercises

Here are some additional things to think about and exercises you can do. If you're not currently in a relationship, think about a recent or important one. Some exercises can be done with your partner. If you're not comfortable doing these at this stage, or if your partner is uncooperative, these questions can give you some cues as to what you may want to talk about with a counselor, should you seek professional help.

1. What "type" of person are you drawn to? For example, an explorer, professor, or someone artistic, religious, or successful? Does that persona represent an unexpressed part of you? If so, what steps can you take to develop that side of yourself? If it describes you or how others see you, do you acknowledge that part of yourself?

2. What first attracted you to your partner? What did you eventually learn about him or her that significantly disappointed you? Did you see evidence of it early on, but ignored it? Was your perception distorted because your partner met some of your needs? Sometimes, the very thing we initially like in someone turns out to be what we dislike.

3. List the traits of your partner that you like and those you don't like. Do any of them remind you of one of your parent's traits? Write about recent positive and negative experiences with your partner that remind you of your memories of that parent. Are you reacting to the negative incidents in the same way you did as a child? How effective is your response? Would you advise a friend to handle a similar situation in the same way?

4. What were your most pervasive positive and negative feelings in your childhood? Do you feel them often in your relationship with your adult self? With your partner? Consider how you may be contributing to these feelings.

5. Think of your unmet childhood emotional needs. Which one did you miss the most? For example, being understood, nurtured, respected, or held. How important is this need to you in your relationships today? Is it still missing? Are your expectations reasonable?

6. Compare with your partner the need that's most important to each of you. Write specifically what actions would fill that need and share the list with each other. Are you each willing to meet your partner's needs?

7. Here is a simple but powerful exercise to build relationship assertiveness skills. Take turns with your partner (or friend) making simple "I" feeling statements *only* about yourselves. Take time to identify the exact feeling. Stop your partner after a few sentences, so that you can remember the words. If necessary, ask for clarification. Repeat back what was said to you, starting with, "You're saying that you . . ." Try to use the exact words that your partner said. Practice on neutral topics frequently, so that when conversations are about more emotional topics, you'll still able to make "I" statements *only* about your own experience and feelings.

8. Notice when you blame or criticize your partner (even if only in your mind) and what your internal feelings are at that moment. Are you perhaps feeling superior or inferior? What would be an authentic "I" feeling statement

you could make? If you're being blamed for something, you could say, "I don't (or I do) take responsibility for that. Please don't blame me." If something is your responsibility, you can admit your error and apologize, but mistakes are human and blame isn't justified. Your partner can learn to be assertive and say, "I feel disappointed (hurt, angry, etc.)."

9. Are you trying unsuccessfully to get your partner to meet your important needs? Do you take responsibility for asking for those needs to be met and fulfilling them on your own to the best of your ability, such as having fun, having hobbies or other stimulating interests, and nurturing yourself? If you've been unsuccessful having your partner meet your important needs, can you nevertheless accept and love him or her? If not, what keeps you in the relationship? What are your options?

Often, sex may be the first thing to go when the relationship is in trouble.[27] Sex can be viewed as a form of communication that mirrors patterns of the couple's other interactions. It also has the potential to expose our most vulnerable, unlovable self and can be powerfully laden with shame on many levels—from body image issues to religious convictions. Chapter 7 provides an overview of sexual self-esteem and shame.

Chapter 7

Sexual Shame

Although sexuality is an integral part of being human, it is often rife with shame and guilt, due to religious, social, and cultural influences. Parents' sexual shame and inhibitions can prevent them from speaking openly about sex and communicating to children that it's natural, fun, and pleasurable. Instead, our sexual needs and behavior, and sometimes even our basic needs for touch and closeness, are frequently shame-bound due to our parents' words, facial expressions, and actions, including punishment and sexual abuse.

Americans have been labeled as coming from the world's most fearful nation when it comes to sex—they do it "queasily, stealthily, guiltily."[1] As a result, most of us don't get accurate information about what's healthy or normal and what's not where sexuality is concerned. About 20 percent of U.S. married couples report having sex six or fewer times per year, and over one-third report having sexual dysfunction issues.[2] Access to contraception is also limited in the United States. Some other Western countries, where sex is culturally treated as healthy and where comprehensive sex education is provided, have lower rates of teenage pregnancy, abortion, sexually transmitted diseases, rape, incest, and child abuse.[3]

Although American attitudes about sex have progressed significantly since the sexual revolution in the 1960s, guilt and shame still affect how people feel, if not how they act. Some men and women continue to believe that intercourse, oral sex, or other sexual behavior is sinful, and engaging in these activities makes them feel guilty, ashamed, or dirty. These beliefs tell us that our natural desire—stimulated by the brain's pleasure center and something we can't control—is wrong. It can't get much more shaming than that.

Regardless of the catalyst, sex brings abundant opportunities to exaggerate both our vulnerability and our feelings of inadequacy, particularly for us as codependents because of our internalized shame. This chapter presents a brief overview of sexual shame, a subject worthy of an entire book. Listed below are some of the many aspects of sexuality that are linked to shame (in no particular order):

- Body weight
- Sexual performance and skill
- Orgasm
- Masturbation
- Size and appearance of genitalia
- Rape
- Sexual slang
- Words and sounds during sex
- Abortion
- Adultery
- Multiple sexual partners
- Sexually transmitted diseases (STDs)
- Male muscularity
- Body odor, discharge, and taste
- Menstruation
- Body hair
- Talking about sex and genitalia
- Sexual desire
- Pornography
- Sex without love

- Fetishes
- Sexual pleasure
- Gender identity
- Sexual orientation

- Sexual fantasies
- Chastity
- Appearance and nudity
- Sexual molestation

Sin

Many of us associate sex with another three-letter word: sin. Since the time of St. Paul, the Catholic Church has taken a restrictive view of sexuality. Puritan, Calvinist, and Victorian values reinforced this view in America, where eighteen states still have laws on the books making oral sex illegal. Until the Second Vatican Council in 1965, the Catholic Church considered sexual desire and pleasure to be sinful, and intercourse was tolerated only for procreation.[4] The effect of this view in patriarchal societies, especially in Latin America and other heavily Catholic regions, promoted an attitude that sex and pleasure were sinful only for wives, which meant husbands were free to seek pleasure through affairs and prostitutes.[5] Despite continued sexual liberation since the 1960s, old sexual attitudes linger and are often significantly different from our behaviors, which contributes to our guilt and shame. Almost all Americans, for instance, engage in premarital sex, yet one-third of Americans and 76 percent of young evangelicals believe it's immoral[6]—an attitude shared by nearly all Asian, Middle Eastern, and North African Muslims.[7]

Masturbation

For centuries, the Catholic Church proclaimed masturbation to be a serious sin. This attitude fueled superstitions, associating it with insanity, fetishes, homosexuality, and the cause of various illnesses and conditions. Other Christian denominations and religions have had similar attitudes about this perfectly natural act.

Doctors recognize that to have healthy sexual and personal development, a child needs to claim separate ownership of his or her body. Self-stimulation is an essential part of this process and may begin in toddlerhood. It becomes more overt in adolescence, especially for boys. Adolescents who repress masturbation inhibit this essential step toward autonomy, thereby making others responsible for their pleasure.[8]

Even though the medical profession has recently accepted masturbation as a normal part of sexual development, 42 percent of young American adults feel guilty about engaging in it.[9] Talking about it is still taboo. In 1995, U.S. Surgeon General Joycelyn Elders was fired for recommending masturbation to reduce the spread of HIV. Nearly all men masturbate, but talking about it makes most of them uncomfortable, despite their denial of any shame.[10] The result is that children learn about masturbation from peers, not parents, and this can add to their shame and misinformation. Even those who aren't ashamed groundlessly worry that too much masturbation harms their sexual functioning.

Fantasy

Sexual fantasies are also a part of normal development. Many of us are ashamed of fantasies about sexual behavior that we might consider immoral, such as having sex with a friend's spouse or being forced into sex, but these kinds of fantasies serve a purpose. The former is a wish based on a natural attraction that we don't act on, typically thanks to our own morality. The latter removes our personal responsibility from the act, which helps us to overcome our sexual shame, fear, and guilt. Psychiatrist and researcher Robert Stoller suggests that sexual fantasies provide a method of converting the pain and shame of our childhood experiences into pleasure and empowerment.[11] A case in point is my client Marjorie. As she recovered from her shame of having been sexually abused and became more empowered, her masochistic fantasies changed to commanding a tribe of male warriors to pleasure her.

Abortion

Abortion is not only a controversial political and social issue but a major cause of guilt and shame, especially for women. An abortion is a difficult enough decision for a woman, who must additionally deal with stigmatization, shame, and secrecy. Although the teen pregnancy rate is dropping predominantly due to evidence-based programs,[12] over one-fifth of American pregnancies end in abortion.[13] A lack of comprehensive sex education due to shame contributes to the high number of unwanted teen pregnancies, particularly in the Bible belt, where comprehensive sex education classes are consistently being phased out of the school curriculum.[14]

Years after the procedure, many women grieve the death of the child they aborted and must heal their guilt and shame. My friend Jan insightfully recounted the devastating trauma she suffered unnecessarily as a teenager due to the shame that caused her to hide her real self for decades:

> *Tom was my teenage romance, filled with excitement, experimentation, and passion. We shared a deep physical, emotional, and spiritual connection that ended in a clandestine Mexican abortion, which was then illegal in the States and in Mexico. Afterward, I wanted nothing to do with Tom, erased my love for him, and pretended to be a virgin again. When we reconnected on Facebook fifty years later, I discovered that that secret abortion had been directing the story of my life.*

I had unconsciously made a decision to live from my intellect, which began driving the car in which I lived. I led the life of an innocent ingénue and college co-ed, but lurking beneath my "good girl" façade was someone else. Shame had cut me off from being a whole person, and it marginalized expression of my lost energies. My suppressed "self" held my creativity, receptivity, vulnerability, sexuality, my capacity to give and receive love, and my need for the kind of full relationship I'd enjoyed with Tom. For fifty years, I'd functioned with only part of me, sort of like eating only the egg whites, but never fully indulging in a healthy egg salad. I was a powerful woman, yet was operating on half of my engine. If I hadn't felt guilty having sex, I might have fought for myself.

This realization was devastating. I cried every day for weeks—not only for the lost child, but for the decades I'd lived without all of myself. I'd suffered a severe undiagnosed and untreated case of PTSD and did not get pregnant again. It's only now that I'm putting it all together and making sense of the devastating impact of that trauma on a young girl.

Homosexuality

Homosexuality has, until recently, been a subject too shameful to be discussed publicly. To counteract this shame, the Gay Pride movement began organizing marches in the 1970s in protest of homophobia. Although there is growing acceptance of homosexuality, fear and repulsion still permeate our society, and many mainstream religious traditions haven't changed their position on gay and lesbian sexual behavior.[15]

Most children born to opposite-sex parents grow up with the expectation of being heterosexual—to have the same sexual orientation as their parents and to love and desire the opposite sex—a view that many parents share. This is part of the child's ideal self. It can be confusing and frightening for these children to discover that their sexual orientation isn't what they expected. As a result, they often develop shame and a sense of secrecy. Children may repress their sexual orientation entirely or struggle against it in isolation. I've treated homosexual patients who have suffered silently for decades and listened to sermons condemning them to hell. In most cases, this suffering occurs in an environment of dysfunctional parenting, where shame and, often, abuse have already taken their toll on a child's fragile developing sense of identity.

Adolescence brings with it even more suffering about being different. Teens are especially sensitive to being accepted by their peers, and many are also establishing their ability to be sexually intimate with the opposite sex. Having little or no sexual experience, they're often confused, afraid, and ashamed about their sexual orientation—even their sexual gender identity. They just want to be "normal"—like their parents and peers. Many of them experience bullying and shaming at school. Some boys are called "a sissy" or "Mama's boy," even by their homophobic fathers. Whereas signs of femininity in boys are frequently frowned on, physical closeness between girls, as well as "tomboy" behavior, is more accepted. Ridicule and social stigma are significant factors in the disproportionate number of adolescent suicides among lesbian, gay, bisexual, and transgender (LGBT) youths.[16]

Due to this ongoing stress, discrimination, and social stigma, those in the LGBT community are more than twice as likely to turn to substance abuse than their heterosexual friends.[17]

When the U.S. Supreme Court overturned the Defense of Marriage Act in 2013, blogger Shaun Sperling wrote about the effects of shame on homosexuals:

No matter where you come from, who your family is or what you do, if you fall within the broad classification of "LGBTQ"—you live under a veil of shame . . . The realization of being different and the fear of rejections plague us and follow us in every area of our life—no matter how hard we fight it. And whether our difference is accepted, celebrated, rejected, or ignored, shame manages to rear its ugly head. I'm not even sure that shame can be removed completely from our beings because it has affected us so deeply—physically, emotionally and spiritually.[18]

Sex and Exposure

Sex is a powerful instinctual drive that compels us to procreate. In its throes, we may release civilized inhibitions against nudity, exposure of genitalia, and losing control of voice and body. Sex renders lovers vulnerable at a depth not shared with even their closest friends. Unlike most other animals, however, humans, with our capacity for shame, tend to prefer sex under the covers and in the darkness.

Shame becomes heightened around sex when there's more to lose—when a lover cares and wants to be loved, and a partner's opinion matters. It makes lovers particularly shy as they approach sex for the first time. For people who have casual sex, excitement and pleasure often overpower any feelings of shame. After sex, these partners—who don't have a friendship or a deeper connection—usually withdraw. But when two people are in love, there is much more at stake. They each want to be desired, and it's always possible that one lover won't be willing, engaged, or satisfied, which opens the other up to the shame of rejection.

People who have a sexually transmitted disease (STD) often feel ashamed, damaged, or marked. They must grapple with the obligation to disclose it at the risk of terminating a budding romance and the possibility of love and sexual closeness. Shame anxiety induces many people to postpone telling the truth about having an STD and therefore risk infecting their partner, losing his or her trust, and ruining the relationship.

The more we anticipate shame, the more we avoid having sex, and this affects the rest of the relationship. Shame and guilt also impair pleasure through reduced sexual desire, sexual inhibition, problems with orgasm and performance, and distracting thoughts during sex. Anxiety about having sex can make partners switch off feelings and sensations and instead participate in the role as an observer by detaching—sometimes called "spectatoring"—or produce obsessive, intruding thoughts, which detract from sexual enjoyment and functions.[19] The Critic's voice during sex can destroy our spontaneity, arousal, and any possibility of authentic connection and enjoyment.

Sexual Identity

Sexual self-schema, or sexual identity (as distinct from gender identity), begins in infancy. It refers to the way we think about our sexuality, ourselves as sexual beings, and our standards and expectations. It begins with how a mother holds, caresses, and nurses her baby, all of which can produce numerous pleasurable sensations—suckling in particular can produce pleasure. The same holds true for the father's touch. Even how parents clean their baby's genitals can communicate their attitudes about him or her as well as their views on sexuality. Our sexual self-schema is defined by the degree of openness, warmth, directness, and romance we exhibit.

Positive sexual self-schemas are associated with positive sexual attitudes, confidence, arousal, desire, pleasure, masturbation, better sexual functioning, and longer-lasting relationships;

negative sexual self-schemas, on the other hand, are characterized by such things as guilt, shame, rigid and unrealistic beliefs, inexperience, sexual aversion, conservative attitudes, self-consciousness, anxiety, less sexual satisfaction, and risky sexual behavior in women, such as not having safe sex.[20] Our Critic can be especially harsh when it comes to our appearance and our sexuality, and negative expectations can become self-fulfilling prophecies, significantly affecting our performance and decreasing our desire and arousal. If our Critic tells us that we're unattractive, that we won't be able to achieve orgasm or satisfy our partner, or that our sexual feelings or certain sexual acts are "dirty," our ability to enjoy sex is diminished, "proving" the Critic right.

Physiology also impacts our sexual self-schema. Men and women develop differently, anatomically and hormonally, affecting identity and approaches to sexuality. Donald Nathanson suggests that a boy's solution to his embarrassing, often visible, sexual arousal is to blame girls for his sex drive, resulting in a tendency to attack others; in response, girls feel guilt and learn to blame themselves.[21]

Women

Women, more than men, tend to have negative attitudes about sex. The Puritans feared women's sexuality and viewed their bodies as a "pollution of evil" that needed to be controlled, often accusing women of sinfulness, heresy, or witchcraft.[22] Later, Victorian attitudes further restricted women by emphasizing restraint and chastity and promoting the belief that both women and children were sexless. In the nineteenth century, women who were considered promiscuous were tested and imprisoned for carrying venereal disease.[23]

Many girls are still taught that they don't have or shouldn't have sexual needs, and consequently nearly three-fourths of teenage girls regret having had sex compared to 55 percent of boys, inferentially due to more guilt and shame among girls.[24] This double standard judges women more harshly than men for premarital sex, out-of-wedlock pregnancy, adultery, and "excessive" sexual desire and partners,[25] all of which contribute to women's sexual shame and negative sexual self-schema.

In contrast, our society tends to encourage male dominance and promiscuity, which debases both sex and women. For example, in the past, the word *vagina* was taboo and "draped in shame," and still today, derogatory sexualized slang is used to criticize powerful women.[26] At the same time, romance and love are idealized by the media; as a result, teens often have trouble distinguishing sex from love. Some young women feel pressured to sanctify their sexual appetite by marrying the boyfriend with whom they're sexually involved.

Because of the societal shame and taboos around sexuality, particularly for girls, it's rare for a parent to talk about sexual pleasure as something that is natural and to be enjoyed. If anything, parents prefer to discuss dangers—such as pregnancy and avoiding disease. As a consequence, many girls learn about their bodies and sexuality by experimenting with eager teenage boys and young men, who are often inexperienced themselves and are often focused on their genitals and a quick orgasm. Some boys pressure girls to have sex. Codependent girls and young women with low self-esteem have difficulty saying no to unwanted sex and may feel guilty for not satisfying their boyfriend. When they do have sex, they don't value their own sexual needs. They learn not to expect much, which can contribute to their inability to achieve orgasm and their feeling inadequate.[27]

Society also places tremendous pressure on women and girls

as young as nine years old to be beautiful, thin, and acceptable, compromising their self-esteem at an early age. By puberty, girls are often self-conscious in the presence of others about the development and size of their breasts, which all can see, particularly in gym class. To some girls, their worth is measured by the size of their bra—whether they need one too soon, too large, too small, or too late. A girl's first period can also be a shame-filled experience. When I was growing up, menstruation was referred to as "the curse." By not talking candidly about it, mothers pass on shame to their daughters, who then hesitate to disclose when their menses begin. Young girls sometimes face humiliation and embarrassment when they first buy sanitary napkins and tampons, refuse to swim at parties, or uncontrollably stain their clothing. It doesn't end there. All of this is re-experienced with each new sexual partner, plus additional fears discussed in the following paragraphs.

Women often feel shame about their facial beauty, their hair, and their body's size, shape, and weight, even if these fall within the "normal" range. They worry whether their vagina will be ready to respond to sexual intercourse and whether they'll be able to orgasm. Shame and a negative sexual self-schema may encourage them to avoid sex or not assert themselves in sexual situations. Shame can decrease their ability to experience orgasm, sexual pleasure, and sexual satisfaction. During sex, many women continually try to avoid being seen and may remove themselves emotionally and psychologically by "checking out" and becoming an uninvolved spectator. Shame thus prevents them from acting assertively in their own interests, potentially exposing them to risky sexual encounters, particularly for younger women.[28] In contrast, healthy self-esteem and satisfaction with her body paves the way for a woman to experience increased sexual desire, confidence, orgasms, and pleasure during sex. She's more assertive and engages in less risky behavior.[29]

Because of fear and shame, a woman can be rigid and controlling, limiting experimentation or ways of pleasing her mate. She may place responsibility for her pleasure on her partner and be sexually demanding. If she's ashamed of masturbating, she may not be aware of what arouses her and expect her partner to "read her body," just as she assumes her partner can read her mind. Such unreasonable expectations breed self-pity and resentment and unfairly burden her partner with the responsibility for her orgasm or lack of pleasure. Her attitude may stem from hostility toward sex or experiences with past partners.

Men

Boys' vulnerability differs from that of girls, in part because a boy's genitals are external, and very early in life he can experience an erection and become self-conscious and ashamed if it shows beneath his clothing. Boys begin masturbating before girls do, often believing it's wrong and shameful. When slow dancing, adolescent boys are frequently ashamed of their uncontrollable and apparent arousal, which they'd rather hide. An unexpected ejaculation would be mortifying. To evaluate their manhood and potency, they might compare the strength and sound of their urine stream or the speed of ejaculation in "jerk circles." Alternatively, they might test their "strength" by attempting to refrain from orgasm when another boy strokes their penis. Passage into manhood often exposes boys to the worst possible humiliation during a period when vulnerability and honesty simply aren't allowed.

As treacherous as sexual encounters are for women, for men, their vulnerability is at stake, and their manhood is tested and subjected to scrutiny with each sexual encounter. They develop muscles to enhance their sexual appeal. Like women, but to a lesser degree, a man's sexual confidence is also related to his body size, muscularity, and weight. If he is ashamed of his body, he can become anxious and self-conscious during sex, with less arousal, desire, and orgasmic satisfaction.[30] Men who approve of their bodies tend to masturbate and have sex earlier in life than those who are ashamed of their bodies. They also tend to have higher self-esteem, and are happier and less anxious and depressed.[31] Like women, men's feelings of sexual inadequacy can lead to lack of desire and a preoccupation with performance and the ability to achieve orgasm.

From an early age, men are pressured to measure up to the masculine ideals of toughness, success, and antifemininity.[32] These values are reinforced by activities such as "girl watching," having a beautiful girlfriend or wife as a "trophy," and addiction to pornography. Although countless men are socialized to be promiscuous and sexually competitive (to "score"), and to objectify, dominate, and degrade women (usually in the presence of other males), half of heterosexual men feel shame about these types of behavior, leading them to question their worth and lovability as human beings.[33]

Depersonalizing sex and objectifying women absolves men of responsibility for their actions and protects them from the shame of rejection.[34] Men want connection as much as women do, but many have been shamed for showing tender feelings, which don't conform to the masculine ideal of toughness. All of these expectations distance men from and generate conflict with their feelings and real self. Thus, sex becomes a substitute for, and is confused with, real intimacy, which for many men is frightening and carries shame anxiety.

Fear of intimacy (for the reasons discussed in chapter 6) is often the source of sexual dysfunction. Sometimes a man who is confident about his sexual prowess is suddenly unable to maintain an erection once a new relationship becomes serious—when his partner's feelings matter or when he begins to feel trapped. Because heterosexual men often gauge their self-esteem, competence, and masculinity on their performance and women's sexual responsiveness, they fear women's sexual power in a domain that's been the basis of their own security and worth.[35] They can become preoccupied with fears of premature ejaculation or being unable to maintain an erection or satisfy their partner. They anxiously monitor and evaluate themselves during sex, diverting their attention from sensual pleasure and impairing their own functioning and enjoyment as well as those of their partner. Although the cause of sexual dysfunction can be physiological, it is usually emotional, stemming from shame anxiety about anticipated failure to perform sexually and the resulting humiliation.[36] Internalized shame and measuring performance against an imaginary ideal of perfection only exacerbate their problems.[37] Unrealistic expectations set in motion a worsening, self-reinforcing cycle, where sexual shame becomes generalized to the whole person, as shown in Figure 7.1.

Perfectionism can prevent a man from authentically relating to his partner because he's busy trying to prove himself. Any experience that isn't "perfect" is a tremendous blow and results in the same anxiety and shame from which it stems. He reacts by being self-absorbed and distant. Some of these perfectionists prefer to abstain from sex or substitute pornography rather than fail. Or, they only approach a partner they aren't emotionally vested in.

The antidote for self-consciousness is to "Lose your mind, and come to your senses." Focus on sensation. This was the solution suggested by the famous sex researchers Masters and

Figure 7.1

**Negative Cycle of
Sexual Performance Anxiety**

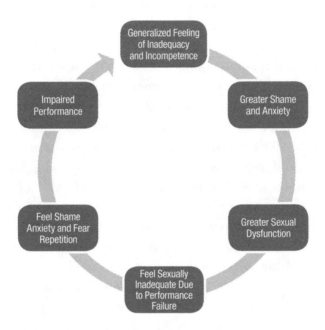

Johnson, who called this process *sensate-focusing.*[38] To start, couples can agree not to have intercourse or even touch genitals. When they're able to experience pleasure, they can then move on to genitals and eventually intercourse if they would like, but without the emphasis on orgasm.

Sexual Abuse

Sexual abuse is not limited to incest, rape, or molestation. It can also include inappropriate kissing, looks, touches, flirting, nudity, or voyeurism, as well as other ways that sexual boundaries are improperly crossed, such as when a parent tells sexual jokes or shares personal sexual material with a child or teenager. Survivors of sexual abuse have been exploited, controlled, and betrayed, often by someone they trusted. Although victims are innocent, they typically take on the shame and guilt of the perpetrator and feel dirty, damaged, and filled with self-contempt. Shame makes them hypersensitive, and they feel awkward, lonely, and unlovable.

Experiencing sexual desire and pleasure rather than obligation is often laden with shame and fear, so much so that some survivors inhibit their desires and deny themselves pleasure, including masturbation. They may have falsely equated being sexually desired with being loved. It may have been the only form of nurturing they ever received, or the only way they could feel close to a parent or other relative. Because they were used and unprotected, survivors have difficulty setting boundaries and may continue to engage in unwanted or degrading sex, believing that it's the price they must pay for love or for being in a relationship. Their fears and needs challenge their ability to have intimate relationships. Sometimes they reject someone in order to prevent being rejected themselves.[39] They need to reclaim a sense of control over their body, which has been stolen. Partners can experience frustration while trying to accommodate the survivor's need for control without feeling shame and responsible for wounds inflicted by someone else.

Self-Esteem and Sexual Self-Esteem

Sexual self-esteem is how we think of ourselves as sexual beings. Do we see ourselves as sexually appealing or unappealing? Do we see ourselves as competent in bed or incompetent? The higher our sexual self-esteem, the more likely we are to enjoy sexual experiences. Although sexual self-esteem is sometimes considered its own distinct category, it is influenced by general self-esteem and vice versa. Any type of abuse that damages self-esteem also lowers sexual self-esteem.

Sex is a form of communication. Codependents find it difficult to be open and direct in their communication in general and even more so on vulnerable topics such as sex. We tend to hide our feelings and needs and attempt to control or please, which often translates into less freedom in the bedroom. As discussed in chapter 6, assertiveness builds self-esteem, and self-esteem enables us to be open, be honest, make choices, and set boundaries, allowing for increased intimacy, spontaneity, and resiliency to shame. Sexual assertiveness goes beyond self-disclosure to actively making requests and initiating action that inherently involves greater risk of rejection.[40]

The ability to freely talk about and initiate sex enhances our sexual self-esteem. In fact, sexual assertiveness and feeling autonomous and empowered are considered key factors in high sexual self-esteem.[41] Assertiveness and self-respect allow us to set boundaries, to say no to unwanted and demeaning sexual behavior, and to express our sexual needs, which are thereby more likely to be met. Studies demonstrate that girls often have sex when they don't want to, but girls with high self-esteem are better able to say no to sex they don't want.[42] Positive sexual experiences produce greater sexual satisfaction and feelings of being valued in a mutually caring relationship, enhancing both self-worth and sexual self-esteem.

Sexual Withdrawal

Partners who repeatedly decline to have sex or who never initiate sex may be doing so out of hurt, anger, or low sexual self-esteem. To avoid having sex, they might manufacture a conflict that makes their partner withdraw. A passive-aggressive husband who lacks desire may do this to preserve confidence in his virility and sexual self-esteem. Codependents may withdraw sexually due to fears of intimacy, losing autonomy, or being smothered. A male Under Dog may retreat if he feels overly pampered. Male and female Under Dogs may resent or lose interest in their Top Dog partner if they imagine she or he feels judged. Shame about drug addiction or alcohol-induced impotency can also cause withdrawal. The Top Dog may be disgusted by his or her partner's drunkenness and withhold sex out of resentment as a form of punishment. It's normal for sexual interest to wane during times of external stress, such as an illness or death, work stress, caring for young children, financial setbacks, or other circumstances that may cause one or both partners to experience fatigue, low mood, or irritability. This is different from sexual withdrawal because interest typically returns when the stressful event passes.

Whatever the reason, withdrawal and disruption of emotional closeness can harm our sexual self-esteem. We need to discuss our underlying feelings with our partner before we can address any sexual issues.

Love versus Sex

Many men, and to a lesser degree women, separate love and sex. They may use sex as a substitute for love and to avoid the anxiety of intimacy. It fills their emptiness, lifts their depressed feelings, and validates their self-worth. Sex may be divorced from all feeling and become machinelike when a wife, for instance, submits because she feels she should or because it confirms her husband's masculinity. Sex without love may be used to allay our anxiety and build identity; however, it can set the stage for impotence and depression later.[43] Even though both partners may be sexually gratified, they're often not fulfilled, nor does their self-esteem benefit. Sex without love can potentially leave both partners feeling more ashamed and empty than before.

Rollo May argues that by putting sensation above passion "we have robbed sex of its power by sidestepping Eros, and we have ended by dehumanizing both."[44] When this is a persistent pattern in an imbalanced relationship, where love and affection are not reciprocated, the partner in love will feel resentful and devastated when the relationship ends.

Men and women are capable of behaving shamelessly in the area of sex. The macho man who participates in dominating risky behavior and the scantily clothed seductress use power over their partner to bolster their low self-esteem and soothe their deep feelings of shame. Sexually flirting with someone outside of our committed relationship can elevate our sexual self-esteem, but at the risk of hurting our partner and damaging mutual trust.

Sexual Addiction

Sex can take on a compulsive quality when it's used to meet other unconscious compulsive needs, such as the need to be loved to allay anxiety or to provide a sense of power and mastery.[45] While it's not currently considered an addiction by the American Psychiatric Association, obsessive and compulsive sex can have the same biological and behavioral criteria as drug addiction and compulsive gambling, and there has been success in treating it using programs such as Twelve Step recovery. Usually, sex addicts discovered sex at an early age, either through sexual abuse or growing up in a highly sexualized environment. In such an atmosphere, children often use masturbation or sex play to self-nurture feelings of abandonment, shame, and loneliness, just as people in other families might turn to food for comfort.

Sex became fused and confused with nurturing. As with all addictions, shame is at the root of sexual addiction.

If children's sexuality was shamed in their childhood, their self-loathing and inner conflict can become unbearably magnified. As adults, sex becomes the center of their world, a source of energy and a remedy for pain and anxiety, and it becomes the primary relationship in lieu of emotional intimacy with a partner.[46] It's their most important need, yet they don't believe they can trust or depend on others to fulfill it, which makes them extremely vulnerable and desperate.[47] It's both important to their identity and a defense to their shame. Because they fear being abandoned and feel ashamed, vulnerable, and unlovable, they have to hide their obsession. A sexual rejection is deeply humiliating and can precipitate a shame spiral. This leads to lies and manipulation and objectification of their partner, whom they desperately need for validation.

The anger and criticism from the addict's mate can create even more shame and justifies the addict's dishonesty and addiction. Sex becomes the focus of the relationship and the measure of the co-addict's self-worth. Sex becomes a sign of being loved. Thus, when the sex addict's addictive behavior doesn't include the co-addict, it's personally humiliating and confirms their underlying belief of being unlovable and unworthy. This makes them afraid that the addict will find them unattractive or sexually inadequate. Co-addicts blame themselves for the addict's actions and also blame the addict for their feelings. Instead of being assertive, they manipulate by using sex as a reward or punishment, by having unwanted sex to control the addict's activities, or by dressing or acting seductively for attention. Both the addict and co-addict feel deeply ashamed and fear being abandoned.

Sexual Rights

Many people feel they don't have any rights regarding sex and are controlled by the views of their parents or partner. Here are some basic sexual rights[48] to think about.

1. **The right to sexual freedom** means the right to express yourself sexually but not engage in any form of coercion, exploitation, or abuse to yourself or others. For example, you have the right to expect the kind of sex you desire, as long as your partner desires it too and you're not violating the sexual rights of anyone else.

2. **The right to sexual autonomy, integrity, and safety** means the right to say no and to make decisions consistent with personal and social ethics and physical and emotional safety. You have the right to make choices with your body, including saying no to sex and refusing to participate in anything that makes you feel unsafe or devalued.

3. **The right to sexual privacy.** You have the right to expect privacy from your partner when you need it, that you can trust your partner enough to be honest and vulnerable, and to expect that what happens in your bedroom stays there.

4. **The right to sexual equity** means the right to be free from discrimination on the basis of gender, sexual orientation, age, race, class, religion, or disability. You have the right to be treated with respect, and the right to enjoy all of the other sexual rights, regardless of who you are.

5. **The right to sexual pleasure** means the right to enjoy psychological, physical, intellectual, and spiritual well-being, and includes masturbation. You have the right

to enjoy your sexuality without feeling guilty or burdened by it.

The step 8 exercises in chapter 8 will help you to develop
a sense of self-love and compassion, grow your sense of autonomy and sexual self-esteem, and break down your shame
defenses.

Exercises

Before moving on to the next chapter, reflect on the shame
events, beliefs, and self-talk that define your sexual identity and
how these manifest in your relationships. If you're currently in
an intimate relationship, the following are some suggestions to
try with your partner. For more on this subject, see my article
"Sex without Orgasm Can Raise Your Self-Esteem."[49]

1. What do you consider to be your sexual rights? Have
   you expressed them in your relationships? If not, why?

2. Explore each other's bodies using the sensate-focus
   method. Focus your attention by bringing your full
   awareness into your hands and sensations. Take your
   time, relax your mind, and allow yourself to feel. Let go of
   making intercourse and orgasm goals. Take turns giving
   and receiving in order to relinquish any obligatory feeling
   to return pleasuring. Remember that sexuality is more
   than purely physical. Full enjoyment requires presence,
   attention, unhurried pleasure, openness, and surrender.

3. When you lie in front in the "spoon" position, put one
   of your partner's hands on your forehead and one on

your heart. Place your hands over his or her hands. Synchronize your breathing. Change places.

4. Sit in your lover's lap, with your legs wrapped around him or her. Each of you then put your right hand on the other's heart, and your left hand on top of your partner's. Gaze into each other's eyes and breathe in unison. Imagine your bodily fluids and energies joining, traveling up your spine, and exchanging through your eyes, heart, solar plexus, and genitals. Try this imagery during intercourse. Be sure to relax rather than tighten up during orgasm.

5. Journal about your feelings, experiences, influences, and early memories associated with the shame-bound aspects of sexuality listed on pages 158–159. If you're in a relationship, sharing your writing can provide an opportunity for openness and mutual understanding.

6. Write your feelings about any sexual experiences you've had involving abuse, however mild, including times when you exploited or abused a partner yourself. How did it affect your self-esteem, beliefs, and decisions, and how does it impact your sexuality today?

The final chapter lays out eight suggested steps with exercises you can do on your own to recover from shame.

Chapter 8

Eight Steps to Free Your True Self

Because shame is so pervasive, most of us can't begin to imagine all the things that shame is keeping us from enjoying—new relationships, greater intimacy, excitement, creativity, new experiences, and a sense of empowerment and freedom that is foreign to us.

If you've been doing at least some of the exercises at the end of each chapter, you're getting a good sense of the extent to which shame rules your behavior and your life. Letting go of shame opens up a new world for codependents—the world you, as your real self, are meant to experience.

Getting in touch with this new world requires getting into recovery. In recovery, we aim to achieve what's possible, rather than strive to attain the impossible: our ideal version of ourselves. Recovery is a lifelong process of discovery, healing, and maintenance. We start by admitting to shame, accepting that we have shame, and then learning the skills we need to let go of it. We find supportive people we can talk to, people who understand what we're going through. Twelve Step groups such as Al-Anon or CoDA are full of people recovering from shame. Meeting with them is enlightening. A huge burden lifts as we come to understand that we're not alone, that others are going through the same thing we are, and that we can help each other.

Part of recovery is re-experiencing painful feelings from the past and learning new lessons from them. But we don't have to do this alone. We can make leaps and bounds in recovery by working with an experienced Twelve Step sponsor, coach, counselor, or therapist. *Professional help is especially essential if we've experienced trauma, such as abuse.* Some psychotherapists are trained in specific techniques to work with trauma, such as eye movement desensitization and reprocessing (EMDR), guided imagery, and somatic experiencing (SE). Cognitive-behavioral therapy (CBT) has also been shown to help with PTSD. The most important thing is that you feel safe and not judged. Even if you're in therapy, the work you do between sessions can significantly speed and deepen your recovery. Ultimately, your effectiveness and sense of well-being are dependent on how you respond to your thoughts, feelings, and needs on a daily basis.

If you're just beginning your journey, be sure that you don't see recovery as a goal to perfect your ideal self on the path to perfect health. Recovery is a journey of self-discovery rather than a destination. In fact, as you become more aware, you may begin to see more clearly the ways you don't measure up to your ideal—despite how hard you try. Be alert to your Critic judging slow progress or lack of it, which can send you down a spiral of self-judgment, criticism of others, and hopelessness. The realistic goal is self-acceptance.

Once we let go of shame, we need a plan to keep it at bay. We're only human, and it's easy to fall back into old patterns. Twelve Step groups and therapy will help us with this as well.

In addition to outside support, I believe that ultimately we need to take eight essential steps to recover from shame:

1. Find Your True Self

2. Uncover Your Shame

3. Find Your Shame's Roots

4. Disarm Your Shame

5. Confront Your Shame

6. Share Your Shame

7. Build Your Self-Esteem

8. Love Yourself

These are concrete steps you can take to let go of shame. What's more, you can do most of them by yourself. At first they may seem to take a lot of effort, but don't let your inner Critic stop you. Taking these steps can change your life. Sometimes the changes will be subtle. You will wake up one morning and realize that a certain problem or issue is no longer nagging at you. At other times, you will feel lighter, freer, or more empowered.

These steps may be more effective if they're worked in order, but as you learn more about yourself and your shame, the steps will begin to overlap. This is a sign that you're connecting the dots—recognizing a shame attack (part of step 2), for instance, and linking it with its root source (step 3), and then feeling a need to share your experience with a person you trust (step 6). You will be doing a lot of writing, so keep your notebook or journal handy. Some of the exercises are best done every day. Others only need to be done initially and reviewed on occasion, especially if you feel your perspective changing or growing deeper. As you grow in your recovery, you will find yourself coming back to some questions and adding detail.

Step 1: Find Your True Self

Chapter 2 describes five selves: our ideal self, our inner Critic, our devalued self, our persona, and our real, true self. Shame leads us to manufacture four of the selves, which camouflage the real self. Getting to know our real self is a process of uncovering and discovering. It can take time to get acquainted and to formulate opinions and values that are our own. After all, it's been four against one for a while. But once we empower the real self, there's no stopping it.

Take time each day to have an inner chat.
Sit quietly and relax your mind and body. Then ask yourself what you're feeling and what you want today—and for the future. Find out what your body, mind, heart, and soul need— what are they asking for? What steps can you take to meet those needs?

Review each day and write about your personal interactions.
Did you ever avoid saying what you were really thinking or feeling? What kept you from doing so? Did you make decisions based on your values?

Write about your feelings.
Journaling about what we're feeling is very therapeutic and enlightening. Sometimes it's easier to express our feelings on paper. Try not to use a computer. Use pen and paper and sit down to write with the intention of being honest.

What is the highest priority in your life right now?
How does your highest priority make you feel about yourself?
Does your life fulfill you at a deep level? If not, what small steps
would bring about change? What were your aspirations grow-
ing up? Did you get sidetracked when you were pursuing them?
How and by whom?

List your values.
Our values are the things that are important to us. We learn values from parents, teachers, coaches, and our real self. Knowing
our values helps us make decisions that are right for us. For instance, if we're apartment hunting with friends and we know
we value privacy, we can quickly decide that we need to have
our own room and make our intentions clear up front, avoiding
issues down the road. Our values can change over time. Revisit
this list often and be sure to write down your values—not those
of your partner or your parents. Chapter 8 of *Codependency for
Dummies* has many exercises to help you identify your values,
needs, and wants.[1]

Dialogue with your child self (on paper).
Having a conversation with your inner child may sound silly,
but you'll be amazed at what you learn—or remember—about
your true self. Ask your inner child questions by writing them
down with your dominant hand; write your inner child's responses with your nondominant hand. Find out what he or she
likes, dislikes, misses, wants, needs, and enjoys.

Step 7 provides further suggestions to experience your true
self.

Step 2: Uncover Your Shame

Shame is our enemy, and to conquer it, we must know it. Until
we become fully aware of our shame and how it operates in

our life and relationships, it controls us. Our Critic is a manifestation of negative, subconscious tapes that have been running since our childhood. Once we acknowledge the Critic and the internal conflict it creates, we have the upper hand. When we're conscious of it, it can't get away with sneak attacks. If it's only partially recognized, we're still susceptible to shame from within and from others,[2] so it's important to give this step your attention. The following exercises support step 2 by heightening our consciousness of shame and how the Critic reinforces it.

Notice when you're having a shame attack.
Once you're able to recognize a shame attack by doing the exercises in chapter 1, you're ready to use this strategy to stop the attack midstream. Label it, relax, and feel it, but instead of continuing to focus inward, direct your focus outward. View your surroundings. Reassure yourself that everything is okay as it is. Listen to sounds around you and observe something colorful or interesting—such as a tree, leaf, or flower—and observe each color, along with the texture, shadow, lines, and scents. Talk to yourself about what you hear, see, touch, and smell. Observe or do something that absorbs your attention, whether it's physical exercise or precise mental work, such as balancing your checkbook. If you can, go outdoors. This will help you interrupt the negative feelings and thoughts. After the attack passes, write about your experience and analyze it. Your ability to interrupt shame attacks will grow with practice. Before long, you'll be able to curtail them and abort a downward spiral.

Each time you're self-critical, give yourself a signal.
Snap your fingers or use a loving gesture like touching your heart or patting your shoulder. Include "shoulds" as criticisms.

At the end of each day, write all of the negative things your Critic said to you.

You may have a hard time recalling these things when you first try this exercise, but as you build awareness of your thoughts and "shoulds," more will come to you.

Record and clarify instances of when you felt shamed or criticized by someone else—even in your mind.

Don't assume you heard the person right, but be open to the possibility that you misinterpreted or misheard what was said. Ask the person whether they actually said what you remember them saying, and what they meant.

Get to know your inner Critic.

You can get to know your inner Critic the same way you get to know your inner child—by dialoguing on paper. Write questions with your dominant hand and answer with your non-dominant hand. Discover the Critic's name, teachers, and motives, and how it feels about you. Assess your Critic's style and whether it uses the same tactics your parent used to motivate or discipline you. Is your Critic professorial, a name-caller, a relentless fault-finder or nit-picker, always looking to find mistakes and flaws?

List all the things you don't like about yourself.

Start with your physical appearance, and include all areas of your life.

List the "shoulds" and expectations you have for yourself and your family.

"Shoulds" for yourself and others signal that the Critic is at work. For example, do you think you *should* keep your home very orderly, make more money, control a situation, do everything yourself, and never make a mistake, be afraid, cry, or raise your voice? Can you connect any of these "shoulds" and expectations to a criticism?

Examine the beliefs you have that support each criticism and expectation.
For example, for the thought "I shouldn't cry about this," the unconscious beliefs might be "I'm weak. If I show vulnerability, I'll get hurt." The thought "I'm a bad person" might be based on underlying beliefs that say, "No one will love me," "I'll end up alone," and ultimately, "I'm unlovable."

Is there a similarity between what your Critic says to you and what you say or think about others?
Every time you criticize someone (out loud or in your mind), consider whether you might believe the same thing about yourself. Write down some examples.

Interview your devalued self.
You know the drill. Write its voice with your nondominant hand. The devalued self often is the most vulnerable, childlike aspect of ourselves. It's the part of us that's been shamed through false beliefs and statements made to us by others and by our Critic. How old is he or she? Ask your devalued self what it feels like to suffer the Critic's tyranny. What does it need, want, and not want? Imagine what others feel when you criticize them.

Write a dialogue between your Critic and your devalued self.
Let these two duke it out. You—your real self—can be the observer. Notice memories and images that arise. What happened? Who shamed you?

Step 3: Find Your Shame's Roots
Part of healing shame entails understanding where our inaccurate beliefs and messages came from. Perhaps you identified

with some of the examples from your own childhood in reading chapter 2. You may or may not remember being shamed, but shame is passed down in families, not only by words but also through actions, family secrets, beliefs, authoritarian control, and unpredictable or unfair enforcement of rules.[3] Healing may require reliving some painful events—a rewinding of our past—this time with compassionate, informed awareness, and as an empathic witness. We can explore where shame started by doing the following exercises.

List some of the rules you grew up with.
Who made them? Could rules be discussed or challenged? What would happen if they were?

What was the family mythology or identity?
For example, some parents see themselves as rebels, outsiders, underdogs, patriots, or having more clout, money, or religion than their neighbors. What beliefs supported this identity? Did your parents feel better than or less than others? Do you share their views of yourself and others?

List some family beliefs and mottos.
For example: "Blood is thicker than water," "Don't air dirty laundry in public," or "A dollar saved is a dollar earned."

Was there a family secret no one talked about, either within or outside the family?
For example, many families hide or deny addiction, mental illness, or abuse.

Think about how you were punished or disciplined.
Was it fair, predictable, humane, and reasonable? What did you feel about it? What do you feel about it today?

How much control did you have as a child?
What degree of privacy and control over your body, actions, and belongings were you permitted? How did you feel about it? What rights did you feel entitled to? What do you feel about it today?

Did you have a perfectionist parent?
What were his or her expectations of you? Were you over-corrected? How did that affect you?

What behaviors were rewarded or praised? How did you feel about such praise?

What was your role in the family?
How did that role make you feel? What did you have to sacrifice as a result? Are you continuing to play that part in your current relationships? What were/are the detriments and benefits of doing this?

In what ways do you feel you were emotionally abandoned as a child?
If you're unclear about emotional abandonment, you may want to reread chapter 2. Neglect and abuse cause emotional abandonment, but it can also accompany lack of nurturance and chronic feelings of loneliness, invisibility, unimportance, and being misunderstood.

List blaming and shaming messages that you received in your childhood.
Include messages from peers, teachers, relatives, counselors, religious leaders, and others. Recall the childhood shaming experiences that are tied to these messages. (You may want to do this with the support of a sponsor or therapist.) Write as much detail as you can remember, including dialogue, sen-

sations, and your feelings about what happened. If you feel rage at your parent, allow it. Allow whatever you feel to be okay. Then get into a relaxed state. Close your eyes and visualize what happened. See your adult self (or your therapist, sponsor, or another trusted adult) enter the scene, protect and stand up for you as a child, and then lovingly and compassionately comfort and hold your child self. Convey the message that he or she is deserving of love, not shame. (This message is true, even if you broke reasonable rules. Perhaps you needed correction, but not shaming for who you were.) In other words, change the outcome of the scene. Then see it recede further into the distance. If your memories are too frightening or painful, it's best to do this with an experienced psychotherapist.

Afterward, write about your visualized experience and how it affected your beliefs about yourself and decisions in your life. Follow the rest of the steps to challenge those beliefs. How were you harmed and what did you lose? How do those experiences play out in your relationships today?

You might attempt to rationalize or justify what happened. Ensure that your Critic doesn't find opportunities to further criticize or blame you, for example, for being weak or angry, not letting go, or allowing abuse.

Repeat this exercise for as many shaming incidents as you can recall, including in your adult life. If an incident still bothers you, work steps 5 and 6 below. Try repeating this process a few times until the memories and feelings about the incident diminish. Consider seeing a psychotherapist.

Compare the list of shaming messages you made with the words of your Critic.
Which messages have the strongest impact on you?

Give yourself time and space to grieve your past and its consequences in your adult life.

Allow yourself to feel any sadness, anger, or other feelings that arise in answering these questions. Grief happens in several stages, starting with denial, and includes anger and bargaining. Be patient; these feelings may not resolve quickly. Consider sharing your story and feelings with a sponsor or professional. If the feelings continue for many months, see a professional. Have a talk with God or your Higher Power about healing your wounds.

Write a letter to the person(s) who shamed you, recounting what was done to you, how you felt at the time, and how it has affected your life.

Read it aloud, imagining that you're reading it to this person, and share the letter with someone you trust. Don't expect to feel forgiveness immediately. Forgiveness is a process. Forgiving someone doesn't mean you condone what happened; rather, it means you no longer feel hurt or angry. If you want to confront someone who shamed you, it's best to wait until you forgive and accept yourself first, but take care that you don't expose yourself to further shame.

Step 4: Disarm Your Shame

The process of healing our shame includes disarming our inner Critic and taking away its ammunition. Understanding our Critic's motives can help us disarm it. It may be attempting to protect us, but it isn't.

Notice when you withdraw from situations to protect yourself from experiencing shame.

What are the consequences of doing this? What would happen if you chose not to withdraw? Write about your feelings and what you would say that would be honest and vulnerable.

Have you ever insincerely said, "I'm sorry"?
Write about your motivations for doing this and the benefits or detriments of making that choice. What would be a different, authentic response?

In step 2, you listed things you don't like about yourself—your flaws. What were your Critic's intentions, motives, and desires with respect to each of your flaws?
Your Critic may be motivated by a desire to protect you from others' criticism—sort of like, "I'll say it first, so you won't be hurt or disappointed when someone else says it"—or may want to discourage you from taking risks, in order to avoid failure. It may be seeking perfection, because it wants you to be loved or succeed professionally. What is the underlying need or fear? Can you allow the feeling and meet your need in a healthy way?

Dialogue with your Critic about the topics it's trying to "help" you with.
Use the paper method described in step 1: write your questions with your dominant hand and the Critic's responses with your nondominant hand. Topics might include your appearance, career, or character traits. This exercise will help you to uncover your deepest feelings and unmet needs that drive your Critic's disapproval. For example, if your Critic complains that you're fat, the deeper fears might be about your health or being alone or unlovable. Your needs might be to maintain health and be loved—not only by others, but by you. In other instances, your Critic may act as your conscience and condemn you when your behavior conflicts with your values.

Do you use addiction and distraction to avoid shame?
You might distract yourself in a meeting by judging others, for example, or you might distract yourself in a meeting by feeling

lust toward someone because you're feeling vulnerable. Do you use drugs, food, sex, shopping, gambling, fantasizing or obsessing about someone, or some other addiction when you feel down about yourself and your life? What are the consequences? In the future, when you feel a craving, write about your negative feelings and call a sponsor or trusted friend. Ask yourself what you risk by being authentic.

Step 5: Confront Your Shame

When we become more aware of our shame, we're able to change and interpret events independently of childhood experiences. We gain the power to choose what to believe and disbelieve about the ideas that we and others have. We become critical thinkers and can then accept or reject self-criticism or criticism from others. Now that we've uncovered the source of our shame and how our Critic perpetuates it, the next step is to confront our shame-based thoughts. They're usually rigid and based on fear and selective negative information, and they often reflect negative interpretations of events, words, and behavior. In this step, challenge your assumptions and beliefs.

Learn to identify red flags.
Is your Critic exaggerating, misrepresenting, or taking things out of context? Is it guilt-tripping you, labeling, or name-calling—calling you an idiot, for example, because you made a mistake, lazy because you're tired, or selfish because you said no? Is your Critic jumping to conclusions and making negative assumptions? Are there other reasonable explanations for why you didn't get an invitation, a raise, or a certain phone call? These tactics of the Critic are red flags. Feel free to confront your Critic. What would your wiser self say?

Test the validity of your Critic's assumptions and beliefs.
Ask others you trust whether they agree with your Critic's statements and beliefs. For example, one client felt ashamed because she was a waitress and assumed people looked down on servers, but a quick survey proved otherwise. Most people, she discovered, appreciate servers for the difficult work they do.

Practice expecting mistakes.
Intentionally make a minimum of five silly mistakes a day. Create a new habit of laughing at your mistakes.

Call your Critic on its strategy.
Once you're on to your Critic's strategy, it loses its power over you. Call it out. The Critic is criticizing just to criticize, and the process is automatic. That's all it knows how to do. Some Critics use the double-bind method: they're very good at paralyzing you by putting you in constant no-win situations. One person's Critic criticized him for not being with his family on the days he put in extra hours and stayed late at work. But when he didn't stay late, his Critic blasted him for not working hard enough and not being a good provider. Call out your Critic when it puts you in a double bind, where you can't act without being wrong. When you become conscious of this strategy that your Critic uses, you're free to act, because you realize your Critic will never be satisfied. You can also contradict your Critic's accusations with statements such as:

"Thank you. I've heard enough."

"Cut it out!"

"Dad's not around now."

"It didn't work then, and it's not working now!"

"You're living in the past."

"That was Mom's belief, not mine."

For each criticism and belief, ask yourself, "What is the truth?"

- How do you know it's true? Examine actual facts and whether there's objective evidence for the Critic's assumptions (besides labels you've received or interpretations you made of others' words and actions).
- Have there been times when this belief wasn't true?
- Are your beliefs universal truths? Are there people who don't share these beliefs?
- Could there be an alternative explanation or point of view? Is your belief rebuttable? For example, making mistakes or acting in self-interest are part of normal human behavior. The belief that you're alone because you're short is rebuttable: isn't it true that short men and women fall in love and find happiness?

In step 2, you listed the expectations that underlie your criticisms. Challenge these expectations.

- Are your expectations realistic?
- Where and from whom did you learn them?
- What are you expected to do?
- Do your expectations actually benefit you and others?
- How would you behave if you acted as you wanted?
- What would happen if you let go of these expectations?
- Can you release any fear of letting go of them?

Consider the underlying premises of your self-criticisms and expectations.

- Is the Critic adopting rules or standards that aren't yours? Were they values or rules of your parents, culture, religion, or education? Are you adopting someone else's criticism—the opinion of your mate, parents, bullies, or other authority?

- Find out if other people have the same or different opinion and what they base it on. Do you agree?

An opinion is just that. It isn't truth. Other people's opinions are not objective truth—they only reflect their tastes, feelings, beliefs, and life experiences.

Are you blaming yourself for something someone else said or felt?

Sometimes people might blame you for their feelings or actions. Each person is responsible for his or her own feelings and behavior. "He made me do it" would never hold up as a legal defense. A different person might have an entirely different reaction than you do. Similarly, you can't "make" someone feel or act a certain way. For example, if you go to a movie with a friend and afterward comment you didn't like it, your friend might criticize you for being negative and blame you for ruining his or her outing. Someone else might have been curious about your opinion and entertain a discussion about the film. Use this logic with your Critic. Think about other possible reactions.

Write down triggers—occurrences that repeatedly cause you to experience shame and shaming messages.

Create a chart that includes your triggers, thoughts, feelings, beliefs, reactions or defenses, and memories. Connect your triggers, feelings, beliefs, and reactions to childhood shaming incidents. See the examples below. Notice that the third trigger stimulates a shame attack. This is a core trigger that contradicts the ideal self.

Table 8.1. **Example Chart**

Triggers	Thoughts	Feelings	Beliefs	Defenses/Reaction	Memory
1. Call not returned	He's angry. I did something wrong.	Hurt Depressed Fear	I'm bad. I'm unlikable. I caused it.	Anger at him Judge him Withdraw	Father punished me with silence.
2. Made error at work	How could I? I'm so careless.	Anger Embarrassed Anxiety	I'm stupid. I should be perfect.	Overeat Snap at others Work overtime	Mother always critical.
3. Overlooked someone's need	I'm absent-minded. I'm selfish.	Shame, freeze Mortification Panic, exposed	I'm selfish. I'm unlovable. Others' needs come first.	Withdraw Attack self	Mother called me selfish.
4. Clothes don't fit	I'm fat. I look terrible.	Discouraged Hopeless Self-loathing Depressed	I'm disgusting. I'm unlovable. Thinness=love.	Withdraw Stay home Eat Feel more lonely and ashamed	Teased about size at school.

The first example is an external trigger for a childhood memory of a parent punishing with silence or cutting off communication. In the second, an error is an internal trigger for self-judgment, originating with an excessively critical parent. The third trigger might arise externally when you're criticized for being inconsiderate or selfish or, alternatively, might take place internally when you become aware that you thought of yourself first or overlooked someone else's need (for example, a friend's birthday or illness). The shame emanates from childhood experiences that your needs didn't count, combined with shaming messages of being selfish. This is a frequent pattern of children of narcissistic parents. The fourth example comes from deep shame surrounding body image, which may arise in reaction to others' comments or internal self-assessments.

Step 6: Share Your Shame

We all yearn for connection, but shame can cause us to feel isolated, abandoned, and as if we don't truly belong. The antidote is self-revelation—authentically sharing our vulnerability with others. This is at the heart of personal relationships: showing others our real self.

The willingness to be vulnerable, to expose feelings in a safe environment, and to ask for our needs to be met despite feeling shame accomplishes six things:

1. It creates connection.
2. It develops a feeling of acceptance.
3. It increases the humility that undercuts false pride and arrogance. Humility builds strength; false pride and arrogance are fragile.
4. It strengthens the true self each time we're vulnerable.
5. It builds trust in self and others.

6. It provides an opportunity for mutuality and acceptance
   in relationships.[4] In other words, if we're both flawed,
   I can't demand that you be different.

Sharing vulnerability and asking for things we need, such
as nurturing, touch, separateness, and intimacy, take tremendous courage. But once we get in the habit of doing it, we will
feel so grounded and sane that we won't want to turn back to
our old pattern of isolating. It's wise to share with people whom
we consider safe, who are open to listening, and who won't
judge us, give unwanted opinions, or impose their experience
or agenda. They will allow us to express our emotions, without
telling us to get over them. *If you feel powerless or trapped in a
relationship, you probably don't feel safe.*

Membership in Alcoholics Anonymous provides a healing
sense of belonging to alcoholics who often feel like outsiders.
Some people in AA refer to other members as "brothers" or "sis-
ters." Sharing "I am an alcoholic" exposes their shame about
their disease in an atmosphere of acceptance. According to AA
expert Ernest Kurtz, "What the addict is ideally striving for is
perfect invulnerability."[5] But sobriety is based on the principle of members helping one another, as was the case for the
two founders, Bill Wilson and Dr. Bob Smith. This implies that
each member *needs* help—that he or she is not self-sufficient
but a flawed and limited human being, just like other members.

These concepts are true for all Twelve Step programs and
are reinforced by each of the Steps. They encourage self-honesty
and reflection and suggest that members take inventory of their
shortcomings and share them with God or their Higher Power
and others. The Steps also diminish shame about past behavior
by turning it into guilt and asking members to make amends
for their wrongs. Consider attending a Twelve Step meeting,
such as those offered by Al-Anon or Codependents Anonymous

(or Alcoholic Anonymous, if you think you're also addicted to alcohol, or Narcotics Anonymous if to other drugs). Regular meetings can be found in most cities and towns, and most organizations post schedules of their meetings online.

Twelve Step programs are considered by many to be a safe place to share. They employ a rule against crosstalk, meaning others aren't supposed to interrupt or offer advice or opinions after you share. Asking someone to sponsor you is another step toward humility and an opportunity to reveal the more personal matters you don't want to share in a large meeting. It's important that you feel safe with a sponsor. Be aware if your sponsor is judging or shaming you and communicate your feelings. If these issues are not resolved, you can change sponsors.

Sharing at an intimate level with a psychotherapist can provide even deeper levels of healing, particularly if you work on issues from your childhood, including trauma. There isn't adequate time to explore these issues in a Twelve Step meeting, nor is a sponsor trained to do so. It takes time to develop trust with someone in a personal relationship and to open up and share vulnerable feelings.

With whom would you feel comfortable being vulnerable?
Write down names and contact information.

Find one to three Twelve Step meetings you could attend.
Write down the locations and meeting times. Commit to attend a meeting at least five times. If you don't feel comfortable, commit to finding another meeting.

Try being vulnerable with someone you trust.
An easy way to make yourself vulnerable is to admit, on the spot, to making a mistake. Try this with someone trustworthy. How did it feel?

Step 7: Build Your Self-Esteem

It's vital for us to replace negative self-talk with positive self-talk. By affirming ourselves, we're building inner resources and self-esteem. As we strengthen our true self, we become resilient to shame and less dependent. This process involves not only introspection but also taking risks to discover more about ourselves. Being assertive involves risk, which is essential to sharing feelings and communicating needs in a manner that provides empowerment and safety. Essentially, this means taking positions, making requests, setting boundaries, and conveying our own thoughts and feelings without commenting on or evaluating someone else's. Developing our true self and self-esteem also requires taking action by becoming more autonomous: learning skills, accomplishing goals, and having interests, supportive friends, and pleasurable hobbies. In fact, having a good amount of positive friends and feelings can help heal and integrate childhood shame.[6] Here are some suggestions to get started:

Practice making "I" statements to others without referencing "you."
When you're tempted to ask someone a question about their wants, opinions, needs, or feelings, make a statement about your own. For example, "I want to do more things as a family," or "I need to feel supported in my job."

Make a list of goals, including educational and professional goals, and prioritize them for the short term and long term.
Break down your top goal into monthly and weekly objectives and daily action steps.

Consider taking an assertiveness class to bolster your self-confidence.

Praise yourself for your positive traits and actions.
For example, praise yourself for completing a task you've been avoiding, for showing kindness to a neighbor, or for exercising when you didn't want to. Recognize the steps you're taking in healing shame, or the times when you prioritize your own needs and desires.

Create affirmations that contradict your shaming messages.
Write them in the present tense and keep them positive—do not use any negative words such as "not" or "shame." For instance, instead of writing, "I am not stupid," write "I am smart." Post these affirmations where you can see them and say them aloud daily.

Take at least one positive action daily.
Think of some of the things you do that make you feel good about yourself—for example, taking a risk, repairing something, cleaning your house, preparing your favorite meal, or calling a sick friend. You don't have to do something as bold as climbing Mt. Everest. I felt incredibly empowered when I first changed an electric outlet—something I was afraid to do.

Act in accordance with your needs, values, and true feelings.
This builds self-esteem. When you don't act in this way, you build your codependent self and provide ammunition for your Critic.

At the end of each day, write three things you did well.
Compliment yourself for them.

What would be the consequences of changing core shame-based beliefs about yourself?
For example, "I wouldn't weigh myself every day," "I would be more honest with people," or "I would share my opinions in business and association meetings."

Imagine how your life would be different if you really felt deserving and good about yourself.

Picture all the details and allow yourself to fantasize. Now imagine acting "as if it were true" today. Visualize this on a regular basis. Experiment and behave as if it were true. Write about your feelings, beliefs, and fears that stop you.

Complete this sentence.

"If I really believed my (mother/father) loved me . . ." For example, ". . . I would have more confidence," "I would be kinder to myself," or "I could accept my mistakes." Keep adding sentence endings.

Write yourself a letter of encouragement.

Repeat encouraging phrases to yourself daily and add them to the letter.

List your positive traits.

If you find this difficult to do, ask some of your close friends. Keep adding traits to the list whenever you or someone else notices something positive about you.

List some things you feel guilty about and people you've harmed.

Be sure to put yourself at the top of the list. In addition to shame, self-esteem can be destroyed by guilt and resentment toward self or others. Self-forgiveness can open the doors to compassion and self-love.[7] Write a story about incidents over which you still feel guilty. Look at the bigger picture, and analyze your motives, beliefs, needs, and feelings. Are you reminded of triggers from childhood? Note that we often feel guilty for no rational reason other than we didn't meet our own ideal standards. When mistakes you made in childhood weren't met with love and understanding, you didn't learn to be self-forgiving. As a result, you may find it hard to forgive yourself.

Find a way to make amends to anyone you've harmed, unless by doing so you'd be exposing yourself or the other person to greater harm.

Discuss your planned amends with someone you trust before making them.

Step 8: Love Yourself

In recovery, we realize that we will always have problems and imperfections. We see ourselves as we are and accept ourselves "as is"—like it or not. Instead of experiencing shame and self-pity, we recognize that imperfections are part of the human condition. We own all aspects of ourselves—those we like and those we dislike. Things we consider flaws don't make us feel unworthy or unlovable but are opportunities for growth and relating to others and to feel their support. Researcher Karen Horney's hope was that patients would "feel sympathetic" toward themselves "as being neither particularly wonderful nor despicable but as the struggling and often harassed" human beings they are.[8] Twelve Step slogans also encourage self-acceptance and humility: "Progress, not perfection," "Easy does it," "Live and let live," "There but for the grace of God," and "This too shall pass" promote acceptance and are reminders to be gentle with ourselves and others.

Self-love begins with self-acceptance, particularly accepting our needs and feelings, which are integral to who we are. Unlike self-esteem, which is an evaluation that can vary, self-acceptance is steady and unconditional. There's no judgment; we accept ourselves despite ourselves. Self-acceptance works wonders. It helps us to be more self-forgiving and makes it easier for us to let go of self-criticism. Instead of comparing our-selves to our ideal or to others, either positively or negatively, we appreciate our singular individuality. We feel that we're enough as we are, without having to prove or improve, and we gradu-ally stop worrying about what others think. Self-acceptance is what allows us to be authentic, spontaneous, and natural. We can finally relax and allow more of our inner, real self to be seen. When we accept ourselves unconditionally, we have no shame or fear of revealing ourselves.

Whereas acceptance is an attitude, love combines both feel-ing and action. Contrary to what many believe, self-love is healthy. It's not selfish or self-indulgent; it's not egotistic or narcissistic. Erich Fromm correctly pointed out that love is an art form that takes dedication and practice, not something we win or "fall in" to. Rather, being able to love another is a fac-ulty to be developed. It entails effort and begins with learning to love ourselves.

Western society has been influenced by the Christian be-lief that human beings are basically sinful, and thus self-love is sinful. But since the Bible says, "Love thy neighbor as thyself," how can loving our neighbor be a virtue and self-love be a vice? We're part of humanity, and as worthy of love as the next per-son. Many kind or religious people are able to love others but unable to love themselves. Some believe having a high regard for themselves is indulgent, conceited, arrogant, or selfish. The opposite is true. The more we love ourselves, the more we will be able to love others. The inverse is also true; hatred of others can be indicative of self-hatred.

When we love someone, we want to understand their ex-perience and worldview. Rather than pity, which is distancing, we offer our attention, respect, support, compassion, empathy, and acceptance. Our caring involves knowledge, responsibility, and commitment. These virtues aren't compartmentalized, because love isn't divisible. The ability to maintain attention and offer compassion requires discipline and time. Thus, as we develop them, our capacity to love ourselves and others grows. In order to learn something, we must desire it and find it worthy of our effort. Although self-love is certainly an important goal, our society is full of distractions, and its emphasis on speed, performance, and productivity make developing self-love a challenge.

Acceptance leads to self-compassion, which is different from love. Self-compassion enables us to witness our feelings, thoughts, and actions with acceptance, caring, and understanding, as we would when empathizing with another. Self-compassion is expressed with gentleness, tenderness, and generosity of spirit—quite the opposite of self-criticism, perfectionism, and pushing oneself. When most people are stressed, overwhelmed, or exhausted, they attempt to do even more, instead of caring for themselves. If you weren't nurtured as a child, self-nurturing can be absorbed in therapy over time. You will learn to integrate the acceptance and empathy offered by your therapist.

Self-love evolves with individuation and requires faith and courage to take risks and overcome life's setbacks and sorrows. Faith in ourselves permits us to comfort ourselves and face challenges and failures without lapsing into worry or judgment. We develop the capacity to see ourselves objectively and know that we'll survive, despite our present emotions. If you constantly seek validation and reassurance from others, you miss the opportunity to develop these internal functions on your own.

Self-love and self-compassion are feelings and actions that require ongoing practice. We have opportunities to love ourselves throughout each day. Here are some techniques you can implement on a consistent basis:

Spend time alone.
Quiet time is essential to identify and listen to your feelings with sensitivity and empathy.

Listen to your needs and fulfill them.
Spend an entire day, weekly or monthly, following your impulses and needs without judgment.

Meditate.
Along with meditation, yoga and martial arts can also help you learn self-awareness and focus your attention. They help you acquire the ability to witness and contain your emotions.

Honor the commitments you make to yourself.
When you don't, you abandon yourself.

Notice when you feel self-pity or like a victim.
Unlike self-compassion, self-pity has anger and lacks acceptance. Who or what are you angry at? Write yourself (the victim) a caring letter, as in the following exercise.

Imagine your devalued self as a dear friend or child.
Address this part of you in the second person, and write a caring, compassionate letter. Repeat as necessary. Practice this attitude every day.

Learn self-care and nurturance.
They're an important part of self-love, and they're difficult to learn if you didn't receive them growing up. Dialogue with your child self on a daily basis, as you did in step 1. Ask your child how you can best nurture, love, and protect him or her. If you're short on time, you can visualize your child and inquire internally.

Touch.
Touch is a way to express love. It's natural to touch and hold those you love, but it may seem awkward to do this with your-

self. When you're relaxed in your bed or bath, try stroking your inner arm, the back of your neck, and your belly. Put your hand on your heart and feel yourself breathe. These are all methods to soothe yourself when you're stressed, anxious, or sad.

Tell yourself loving messages.
Whatever stress happens during your day, take a deep breath and send yourself loving and kind messages, such as, "I know this is really tough—I am here. I love you."

By caring for your precious, vulnerable self, you become empowered. You stop relying on your defenses or others for your contentment. By loving yourself, you can begin to love and relate deeply and authentically to others.

Appendix: Self-Compassion Test

Dr. Kristin Neff researched self-compassion and developed the following quiz. In answering, think about your behavior as well as your self-talk; for example, ignoring your needs, such as working when you're tired or isolating when you're lonely, wouldn't demonstrate caring toward yourself. Your answers can increase your awareness about areas you want to change. Be sure not to use them as ammunition for your Critic, nor your score as evidence of your inadequacy.

How I Typically Act towards Myself in Difficult Times

Please read each statement carefully before answering. To the left of each item, indicate how often you behave in the stated manner, using the following scale:

Almost never   Almost always

    1   2   3   4   5

_____1. I'm disapproving and judgmental about my own flaws and inadequacies.

_____2. When I'm feeling down I tend to obsess and fixate on everything that's wrong.

_____3. When things are going badly for me, I see the difficulties as part of life that everyone goes through.

_____4. When I think about my inadequacies, it tends to make me feel more separate and cut off from the rest of the world.

_____5. I try to be loving towards myself when I'm feeling emotional pain.

_____6. When I fail at something important to me I become consumed by feelings of inadequacy.

_____7. When I'm down and out, I remind myself that there are lots of other people in the world feeling like I am.

_____8. When times are really difficult, I tend to be tough on myself.

_____9. When something upsets me I try to keep my emotions in balance.

_____10. When I feel inadequate in some way, I try to remind myself that feelings of inadequacy are shared by most people.

_____11. I'm intolerant and impatient towards those aspects of my personality I don't like.

_____12. When I'm going through a very hard time, I give myself the caring and tenderness I need.

_____13. When I'm feeling down, I tend to feel like most other people are probably happier than I am.

_____14. When something painful happens I try to take a balanced view of the situation.

_____15. I try to see my failings as part of the human condition.

_____16. When I see aspects of myself that I don't like, I get down on myself.

_____17. When I fail at something important to me I try to keep things in perspective.

_____18. When I'm really struggling, I tend to feel like other people must be having an easier time of it.

_____19. I'm kind to myself when I'm experiencing suffering.

_____20. When something upsets me I get carried away with my feelings.

_____21. I can be a bit cold-hearted towards myself when I'm experiencing suffering.

_____22. When I'm feeling down I try to approach my feelings with curiosity and openness.

_____23. I'm tolerant of my own flaws and inadequacies.

_____24. When something painful happens I tend to blow the incident out of proportion.

_____25. When I fail at something that's important to me, I tend to feel alone in my failure.

_____26. I try to be understanding and patient towards those aspects of my personality I don't like.[1]

Average your scores for the following topics:
Self-Kindness: Questions 5, 12, 19, 23, and 26
Self-Judgment: Questions 1, 8, 11, 16, and 21
Common Humanity: Questions 3, 7, 10, and 15
Isolation: Questions 4, 13, 18, and 25
Mindfulness: Questions 9, 14, 17, and 22
Over-Identification: Questions 2, 6, 20, 24

Score interpretations:
As a rough guide, a score of 1–2.5 for your overall self-compassion score indicates you are low in self-compassion, 2.5–3.5 indicates you are moderate, and 3.5–5.0 means you are high. For the Self-Judgment, Isolation, and Over-Identification topics, reverse your score (1=5, 2=4, 3=3, 4=2, 5=1). Lower scores on these dimensions are indicative of more self-compassion.[2]

Notes

Chapter 1

1. Ying Wong and Jeanne Tsai, "Cultural Models of Shame and Guilt," in *Handbook of Self-Conscious Emotions*, eds. Jessica L. Tracy, Richard W. Robins, and June Price Tangney (New York: Guilford Press, 2007), 210–23, http://psych.stanford.edu/~tsailab/PDF/yw07sce.pdf.

2. "Tackling South Korea's High Suicide Rates," *BBC News Asia*, November 7, 2011, www.bbc.co.uk/news/world-asia-pacific-15331921; B. C. Ben Park and David Lester, "South Korea," in *Suicide in Asia: Causes and Prevention*, ed. Paul S. F. Yip (Aberdeen, Hong Kong: Hong Kong University Press, 2008), 27–30.

3. Boyé Lafayette De Mente, *There's a Word for It in Mexico* (Lincolnwood, IL: NTC Publishing Group, 1996), 79–80.

4. Michael Lewis, *Shame: The Exposed Self* (New York: Free Press, 1992), 125.

5. Silvan S. Tomkins, *Affect Imagery Consciousness*, vol. 2: *The Negative Affects* (New York: Springer Publishing Company, 1963), 118.

6. Donald C. Klein, "The Humiliation Dynamic: An Overview," *Journal of Primary Prevention* 12, no. 2 (1991): 117.

7. June Price Tangney, Jeff Stuewig, and Debra J. Mashek, "Moral Emotions and Moral Behavior," *Annual Review of Psychology* 58 (2007): 345–72, http://www.ncbi.nlm.nih.gov/pmc/articles/PMC3083636/.

8. Ibid.

9. Robert Karen, "Shame," *Atlantic Monthly*, February 1992, 58.

10. Ibid.

11. Tomkins, *Affect Imagery Consciousness*, 123, 185–86.

12. Ibid., 144.

13. Gershen Kaufman, *Shame: The Power of Caring*, 2nd ed. (Cambridge, MA: Schenkman Publishing Company, 1985), vii–viii.

14. Internalization of shame was first coined by Gershen Kaufman in *Shame: The Power of Caring* (Cambridge, MA: Schenkman Publishing Company, 1980), 8.

15. Tomkins, *Affect Imagery Consciousness*, 302–303.

16. Allen Wheelis, *How People Change* (New York: Harper & Row, 1973), 75.

17. Adapted from Donald L. Nathanson, *Shame and Pride: Affect, Sex, and the Birth of the Self* (New York: W. W. Norton & Company, 1992), 317.

18. William Shakespeare, *Macbeth*, act 1, scene 3.

19. Rollo May, *Man's Search for Himself* (New York: W. W. Norton & Company, 1953), 43.

20. Wheelis, *How People Change*, 73.

21. Ibid., 76.

Chapter 2

1. Maia Szalavitz, "It's the Orphanages, Stupid!" Forbes.com, April 10, 2010, http://www.forbes.com/2010/04/20/russia-orphanage-adopt-children-opinions-columnists-medialand.html. See also www.encyclopedia.com/topic/orphanages.aspx.

2. Gershen Kaufman, *The Psychology of Shame: Theory and Treatment of Shame-Based Syndromes* (New York: Springer Publishing Company, 1989), 33.

3. Leon Wurmser, *The Mask of Shame* (Baltimore, MD: Johns Hopkins University Press, 1981), 167.

4. Darlene Lancer, *Codependency for Dummies* (Hoboken, NJ: John Wiley and Sons, 2012), 97–98.

5. Lewis, *Shame*, 93–95.

6. Tomkins, *Affect Imagery Consciousness*, 74.

7. Karen Horney, *Neurosis and Human Growth: The Struggle toward Self-Realization* (1950; reprint, with a foreword by Jeffrey Rubin and Stephanie Steinfeld, New York: W. W. Norton & Company, 1991), 17 (page citations are to the reprint edition).

8. Wurmser, *Mask of Shame*, 163.

9. Horney, *Neurosis and Human Growth*, 18.

10. Leon Wurmser, "'Abyss Calls Out to Abyss': Oedipal Shame, Invisibility, and Broken Identity," *American Journal of Psychoanalysis* 63, no. 4 (December 2003): 299–316.

11. Horney, *Neurosis and Human Growth*, 21.

12. Christopher F. Monte, *Beneath the Mask*, 2nd ed. (New York: Holt, Rinehart and Winston, 1980), 470–71.

13. Horney, *Neurosis and Human Growth*, 23.

14. Ibid., 24.

15. Lancer, *Codependency for Dummies*, 30.

16. Charles C. Whitfield, *Healing the Child Within: Discovery and Recovery for Adult Children of Dysfunctional Families* (Deerfield Beach, FL: Health Communications, 1987), 28.

17. Wurmser, *Mask of Shame*, 97.

18. Thomas F. Fogarty, "On Emptiness and Closeness," parts 1 and 2, *The Best of the Family* 3, no. 1 (1976): 3–10; 3, no. 2 (1978): 39–49.

19. Adapted from "Self-Discrepancy Theory2," by Christie88, Wikimedia Commons, page last modified April 7, 2012, http://commons.wikimedia .org/wiki/File:Self-Discrepancy_Theory2.jpg.

20. Lewis, *Shame*, 105.

21. Karen, "Shame," 62.

22. Tomkins, *Affect Imagery Consciousness*, 220.

23. Wurmser, "'Abyss.'"

24. Tomkins, *Affect Imagery Consciousness*, 306–12, 350–53.

25. Ibid., 105.

26. Ibid., 111, 317.

27. Ibid., 95–97.

28. Ibid.

29. Ibid., 419.

30. Karen Horney, *The Neurotic Personality of Our Time* (1937; reprinted London: Routledge, 1999), 85.

31. Tomkins, *Affect Imagery Consciousness*, 255.

Chapter 3

1. I don't differentiate among defense mechanisms such as denial and projection, reactions such as aggression and envy, or psychological defenses and compensation such as arrogance and perfectionism. In a general sense, these can all be considered "defenses," and I refer to them as such. There are other defense mechanisms we use for

uncomfortable feelings, thoughts, and behavior; however, this chapter only focuses on defenses that are more specifically used to avoid shame.

2. Linda M. Hartling et al., *Shame and Humiliation: From Isolation to Relationship Transformation* (Wellesley, MA: Wellesley Centers for Women Publications, 2000), 9.

3. Gershen Kaufman, *Shame: The Power of Caring*, 2nd ed., 85.

4. Horney, *Neurosis and Human Growth*, 296–97.

5. Lewis, *Shame*, 153.

6. Tangney, Stuewig, and Mashek, "Moral Emotions and Moral Behavior," 3 (page number is for the online version).

7. Horney, *Neurosis and Human Growth*, 231.

8. Monte, *Beneath the Mask*, 479. Horney referred to these categories as "Expansive Solution," "Resignation Solution," and "Self-Effacing Solution."

9. Søren Kierkegaard, *Fear and Trembling and The Sickness unto Death* (Garden City, NY: Doubleday and Company, 1955), 152.

10. Eric Fromm, *The Art of Loving* (New York: Harper and Brothers Publishers, 1956), 11.

11. Susan Miller, *The Shame Experience* (Hillsdale, NJ: Analytic Press, 1993), 133–34.

Chapter 4

1. May, *Man's Search for Himself*, 27.

2. Alphonse de LaMartine, "L'Isolement," translated by Geoffrey Barto, 2002, http://www.gbarto.com/hugo/isolementlm.xml.

3. Ibid.

4. Coined by Sartre, *existentialism* grew out of the nihilism and alienation of a Godless, post–World War II society and influenced many philosophers, writers, filmmakers, and artists, including Martin Heidegger, Søren Kierkegaard, Rollo May, Paul Tillich, Erich Fromm, Viktor Frankl, Leo Tolstoy, Franz Kafka, Fyodor Dostoyevsky, Ernest Hemingway, T. S. Eliot, Albert Camus, Edvard Munch, and Edward Hopper. Søren Kierkegaard is considered the first existentialist.

5. Gordon E. Bigelow, "A Primer of Existentialism," http://www.mrjeffrey .com/English%20IV/Existentialism/A_Primer_of_Existentialism.doc.

6. Viktor E. Frankl, *Man's Search for Meaning* (Boston, MA: Washington Square Press, 1948), 125.

7. Ibid., 125. See also Clive G. Hazell, "A Scale for Measuring Experienced Levels of Emptiness and Existential Concern," *Journal of Psychology* 117, no. 2 (1984): 177–82.

8. Clive G. Hazell, "A Scale for Measuring Experienced Levels of Emptiness and Existential Concern," *Journal of Psychology* 117, no. 2 (1984): 177–82.

9. James F. Masterson, *The Search for the Real Self: Unmasking the Personality Disorders of Our Age* (New York: Free Press, 1988), 59.

10. Wurmser, "'Abyss.'"

11. It has been suggested that even infants fill the absence of their mother with "no-breast" negative thoughts or longing for their mother. Neville Symington and Joan Symington, *The Clinical Thinking of Wilfred Bion* (London: Routledge, 1996), 82–83.

12. Jiddu Krishnamurti, *On Love and Loneliness* (HarperSanFrancisco, 1993), 56.

13. Geneen Roth, *Women Food and God: An Unexpected Path to Almost Everything* (New York: Scribner, 2010), 53–54.

14. Susan Kleinman and Jennifer Nardozzi, "Hunger of the Soul in Eating Disorders: Insight from The Renfrew Center," 2010, http://blogs .psychcentral.com/weightless/2010/11/hunger-of-the-soul-in-eating -disorders-insight-from-the-renfrew-center/.

15. Ibid.

16. Sandy Richardson, with Susan Wilsie Govier, *Soul Hunger: A Personal Journey* (Ozark, AL: Remuda Ranch/ACW Press, 2006).

17. Otto Kernberg, *Aggressivity, Narcissism, and Self-Destructiveness in the Psychotherapeutic Relationship* (New Haven, CT: Yale University Press, 2004), 51.

18. Ernest Hemingway and Sean Hemingway, *A Moveable Feast: The Restored Edition* (New York: Scribner, 2010), 48.

19. Ibid., 52.

20. Masterson, *Search for the Real Self,* 74.

21. Darlene Lancer, "Recovery in the 12 Steps: How It Works," *The Therapist* (November 2004): 68–69, also available at http://www .whatiscodependency.com/recovery-in-the-12-steps-how-it-works.

22. Fogarty, "On Emptiness and Closeness," part 1, 7–9.

23. Roth, *Women Food and God*, 57.

24. May, *Man's Search for Himself*, 24.

25. Carl Jung, January 30, 1961, letter in *C. G. Jung Letters*, vol. 2 (Princeton, NJ: Princeton University Press, 1976).

26. Robert Stolorow, "I'll Be with You When the Deal Goes Down," http://www.psychologytoday.com/blog/feeling-relating-existing/201303/i-ll-be-you-when-the-deal-goes-down.

27. Lancer, *Codependency for Dummies*, 231–34.

28. Krishnamurti, *On Love and Loneliness*, 48, 50–53, 96.

29. Ibid., 127.

30. Clive G. Hazell, *The Experience of Emptiness* (Bloomington, IN: 1stBooks, 2003), 19–20.

31. Ken McLeod, "A Way of Freedom," http://www.unfetteredmind.org/a-way-of-freedom.

Chapter 5

1. Horney, *Neurosis and Human Growth*, 43.

2. Lewis, *Shame*, 93.

3. Wurmser, *Mask of Shame*, 192.

4. Etienne Benson, "The Many Faces of Perfectionism," *American Psychological Association* 34, no. 10 (November 2003): 18, http://www.apa.org/monitor/nov03/manyfaces.aspx.

5. Kaufman, *Psychology of Shame*, 75–76.

6. Ibid.

7. *Codependency for Dummies* explores these symptoms and others in greater detail with exercises and tips to overcome them.

Chapter 6

1. Wurmser, *Mask of Shame*, 308.

2. Krishnamurti, *On Love and Loneliness*, 57, 74.

3. Robert W. Firestone and Joyce Catlett, *Fear of Intimacy* (Washington, D.C.: American Psychological Association, 1999), 4–5.

4. Ibid., 7.

5. May, *Man's Search for Himself*, 243.

6. Firestone and Catlett, *Fear of Intimacy*, 311.

7. Ibid.

8. Tomkins, *Affect Imagery Consciousness*, 277.

9. Heinz Kohut, *Search for the Self: Vol. 1: Selected Writings of Heinz Kohut, 1971-1981*, ed. Paul Orenstein (London: Karnac Books Ltd., 2011), 481.

10. Wurmser, *Mask of Shame*, 117.

11. Ibid., 64.

12. Thomas F. Fogarty, "The Distancer and the Pursuer," *The Best of the Family* 7, no. 1 (1978), 13.

13. Horney, *Neurosis and Human Growth*, 240.

14. Ibid., 246.

15. Firestone and Catlett, *Fear of Intimacy*, 25.

16. Ibid., 41.

17. Thomas F. Fogarty, "On Emptiness and Closeness," part 1, 6.

18. Darlene Lancer, "The Dance of Intimacy," 1992, http://www.whatis codependency.com/the-dance-of-intimacy.

19. Lewis, *Shame*, 184.

20. Wurmser, *Mask of Shame*, 203.

21. Horney, *Neurosis and Human Growth*, 245, 252.

22. M. Scott Peck, *The Road Less Traveled* (New York: Simon and Schuster, 1978), 115.

23. Firestone and Catlett, *Fear of Intimacy*, 7, 9.

24. Donald L. Nathanson, *Shame and Pride: Affect, Sex, and the Birth of the Self* (New York: W. W. Norton & Company, 1992), 251.

25. Darlene Lancer, "Your Intimacy Index," 2012, http://www .whatiscodependency.com/intimacy.

26. Ernest Kurtz, *Shame and Guilt*, e-book (Lincoln, NV: iUniverse, 2007).

27. William E. Thornton, *Codependency, Sexuality, and Depression* (Washington, DC: The PIA Press, 1990), 83.

Chapter 7

1. Albert Ellis, *Sex without Guilt* (Fort Lee, NJ: Barricade Books, 2003), 63–64, 93–99.

2. Marianne Brandon, "DEBATE – The Challenge of Monogamy: Bringing It out of the Closet and into the Treatment Room," *Sexual and Relationship Therapy* 26, no. 3 (August 2011): 271–77.

3. Judith Levine, *Harmful to Minors: The Perils of Protecting Children from Sex* (Minneapolis, MN: University of Minnesota Press, 2002), ix.

4. Joan Ohanneson, *And They Felt No Shame: Christians Reclaim Their Sexuality* (Minneapolis, MN: Winston Press, 1983), 37–44.

5. Silvana Paternostro, *In the Land of God and Man: Confronting Our Sexual Culture* (New York: Penguin Putnam, 1998), 83.

6. 88 percent of Americans and 80 percent of young, evangelical Christians ages 18–29 have premarital sex. "Christian Teens Embracing 'Sinful' Sexual Relations," http://www.themonastery.org/blog/2011/10 /christian-teens-embracing-sinful-sexual-relations; "Even Grandma Had Pre-Marital Sex, Survey Finds," Today Health, http://www.today .com/id/16287113/ns/today-today_health/t/even-grandma-had -premarital-sex-survey-finds/#.Uf1cXKzYFjQ; and http://www .transformmn.org/wp-content/uploads/2010/06/Evangelical-Young -Adults-Confused-About-Sex.pdf.

7. "The World's Muslims: Religion, Politics and Society. Chapter 3: Morality," *PewResearch Religion & Public Life Project* (April 30, 2013), http://www.pewforum.org/2013/04/30/the-worlds-muslims-religion -politics-society-morality.

8. Thornton, *Codependency, Sexuality and Depression*, 51–52.

9. Morningside Recovery, "Morningside Recovery Conducts National Survey on Excessive Masturbation," *Boston.com*, February 6, 2013, http://finance.boston.com/boston/news/read/23387951/Morningside_ Recovery_Conducts_National_Survey_on_Excessive_Masturbation.

10. Anne Stirling Hastings, *Body & Soul: Sexuality on the Brink of Change* (New York: Insight Books, 1996), 106–7.

11. Robert J. Stoller, *Sexual Excitement: Dynamics of Erotic Life* (London: H.Karnac Books, 1986), 30.

12. 7 percent of teens became pregnant in 2008, according to "Pregnancy and Childbearing Among U.S. Teens," Planned Parenthood, http://www .plannedparenthood.org/files/PPFA/pregnancy_and_childbearing .pdf. There has been a 52 percent decline in the rate of teen pregnancies since 1991; 29 percent of this decline has been in the last five years (2008–2013). Joshua DuBois, "Teen Pregnancies Drop a Whopping

52 Percent in Two Decades," *Daily Beast,* December 8, 2013, http://
www.thedailybeast.com/articles/2013/12/08/teen-pregnancies-drop
-a-whopping-52-percent-in-two-decades.html.

13. 22 percent end in abortion, of which 43 percent of mothers are
Protestant, 27 percent Catholics, and 13 percent are evangelicals.
"Abortion Statistics," Orlando Women's Center, http://www
.womenscenter.com/abortion_stats.html. See also "Facts on Induced
Abortion in the United States," Guttmacher Institute, October 2013,
http://www.guttmacher.org/pubs/fb_induced_abortion.html.

14. David Sessions, "Evangelicals Struggle to Address Premarital Sex and
Abortion," *The Daily Beast,* July 13, 2012, http://www.thedailybeast
.com/articles/2012/07/13/evangelicals-struggle-to-address-premarital
-sex-and-abortion.html.

15. Ohanneson, *And They Felt No Shame,* 134.

16. In 2008, it was estimated gay, lesbian, and bisexual American youth
were up to 7 percent more likely to attempt suicide than straight
adolescents. "Suicide Risk and Prevention for Lesbian, Gay, Bisexual,
and Transgender Youth," Suicide Prevention Resource Center, 2008,
http://www.sprc.org/library/SPRC_LGBT_Youth.pdf.

17. Jerome Hunt, "Why the Gay and Transgender Population Experiences
Higher Rates of Substance Use—Many Use to Cope with Discrimination
and Prejudice," Center for American Progress, March 9, 2012, http://
www.americanprogress.org/issues/lgbt/report/2012/03/09/11228
/why-the-gay-and-transgender-population-experiences-higher-rates
-of-substance-use.

18. Shaun Sperling, "What the Same Sex Marriage Cases Mean for Gay
Shame," *HuffPost Gay Voices* (blog), June 28, 2013, http://www
.huffingtonpost.com/shaun-sperling/what-the-same-sex-marriag_
b_3517563.html.

19. H. S. Kaplan, *The New Sex Therapy* (New York: Brunner/Mazel,
1974), 132, 220.

20. Hannah J. Davis, Genevieve M. Laliberte, and Elke D. Reissing,
"Young Women's Sexual Adjustment: The Role of Sexual Self-Schema,
Sexual Self-Efficacy, Sexual Aversion and Body Attitudes," *Canadian
Journal of Human Sexuality* 14, no. 3–4 (Fall–Winter 2005): 77;
Femke van den Brink and Liesbeth Woertman, "Body Image and
Female Sexual Functioning and Behavior: A Review," *Journal of Sex*

Research 49, no. 2–3 (March–June 2012): 184; and B. L. Andersen and J. M. Cyranowski, "Women's Sexual Self-Schema," *Journal of Personality and Social Psychology* 67 (1994): 1079–1100.

21. Donald L. Nathanson, *Shame and Pride: Affect, Sex, and the Birth of the Self* (New York: W. W. Norton & Company, 1992), 268, 375.

22. Marilyn J. Westerkamp, "Puritan Women, Spiritual Power, and the Question of Sexuality," in *The Religious History of American Women: Reimagining the Past,* ed. Catherine A. Brekus (Chapel Hill, NC: The University of North Carolina Press, 2007), 61.

23. Emma Brockes, "Naomi Wolf: 'Neural Wiring Explained Vaginal v Clitoral Orgasms. Not Culture. Not Freud,'" *The Guardian,* September 2, 2012, http://www.theguardian.com/books/2012/sep/02/naomi-wolf-women-orgasm-neural-wiring.

24. Levine, *Harmful to Minors,* 136–37.

25. Ellis, *Sex without Guilt,* 134.

26. Brockes, "Naomi Wolf."

27. Ellis, *Sex without Guilt,* 134.

28. Deborah Schooler, L. Monique Ward, Ann Merriwether, and Allison S. Caruthers, "Cycles of Shame: Menstrual Shame, Body Shame, and Sexual Decision-Making," *Journal of Sex Research* 42, no. 4 (November 2005): 324–34.

29. Van den Brink and Woertman, "Body Image," 184.

30. Lorraine K. McDonagh, Brian E. McGuire, and Todd G. Morrison, "The Naked Truth: Development of a Scale Designed to Measure Male Body Image Self-Consciousness during Physical Intimacy," *Journal of Men's Studies* 16, no. 3 (Fall 2008): 253.

31. Patricia M. Pascoal, Hospital Julio de Matos, and Nuno Monteiro Pereira, "Young Men's Body Image Satisfaction and Sexuality: A Comparative Study," *Journal of Sex Research* 43, no. 1 (February 2006): 7.

32. William B. Elder, "The Centerfold Syndrome: Exploring the Constructs of Heterosexual Male Sexual Self-Schemas," Master Thesis (Salt Lake City, UT: University of Utah, 2010), 5–6, http://content.lib.utah.edu/utils/getfile/collection/etd2/id/2047/filename/1330.pdf.

33. Ibid., 122–23.

34. Patrick Carnes, *Out of the Shadows: Understanding Sexual Addiction* (Minneapolis, MN: CompCare Publishers, 1992), 117; William Pollack,

Real Boys: Rescuing Our Sons from the Myths of Boyhood (New York: Random House, 1998), 150–51.

35. Gary R. Brooks, *The Centerfold Syndrome: How Men Can Overcome Objectification and Achieve Intimacy with Women* (San Francisco, CA: Jossey-Bass, 1995), 6.

36. Kaufman, *Psychology of Shame*, 145.

37. Ellis, *Sex without Guilt*, 104.

38. William H. Masters and Virginia E. Johnson, chapter 2 in *Human Sexual Inadequacy* (1970; reprinted Bronx, NY: Ishi Press International, 2010).

39. G. B. Rahm, B. Renck, and K. C. Ringsberg, "'Disgust, Disgust beyond Description'—Shame Cues to Detect Shame in Disguise, in Interviews with Women Who Were Sexually Abused during Childhood," *Journal of Psychiatric and Mental Health Nursing* 13 (2006): 100–109.

40. Dana A. Menard and Alia Offman, "The Interrelationships between Sexual Self-Esteem, Sexual Assertiveness and Sexual Satisfaction," *Canadian Journal of Human Sexuality* 18, no. 1-2 (Spring–Summer 2009): 35.

41. Faith Auton-Cuff, Jose F. Domene, Kristelle D. Heinrichs, and Chuck MacKnee, "Factors Affecting Sexual Self-Esteem among Young Adult Women in Long-Term Heterosexual Relationships," *Canadian Journal of Human Sexuality* 18, no. 4 (Winter 2009): 183.

42. Levine, *Harmful to Minors*, 135–36.

43. May, *Man's Search for Himself*, 105.

44. Ibid., 65.

45. Horney, *Neurosis and Human Growth*, 302.

46. Carnes, *Out of the Shadows*, 16.

47. Ibid., 118, 142.

48. Ellis, *Sex without Guilt*, 226.

49. Darlene Lancer, "Sex without Orgasm Can Raise Your Self-Esteem," 2013, www.whatiscodependency.com/sex-without-orgasm-can-raise-your-self-esteem. See also "Body and Soul: Sex and Spirituality," *Whole Life Times* (October 1991), http://www.whatiscodependency.com/codependent-relationship-addiction-articles/#8.

Chapter 8

1. Darlene Lancer, "Taking Stock of Who You Are," in *Codependency for Dummies,* 119–132.

2. Tomkins, *Affect Imagery Consciousness,* 281–82.

3. See Darlene Lancer, "How Did You Become Codependent?" *Codependency for Dummies,* 97–118.

4. Kurtz, *Shame and Guilt.*

5. Ibid.

6. Tomkins, *Affect Imagery Consciousness,* 342.

7. Read eighteen tips on "How to Overcome Guilt and Forgive Yourself" at http://www.whatiscodependency.com/ho-to-overcome-guilt-and -forgive-yourself.

8. Horney, *Neurosis and Human Growth,* 359.

Appendix

1. Test reprinted from Kristin D. Neff, "Development and Validation of a Scale to Measure Self-Compassion," Self and Identity 2 (2003): 223–50, http://www.self-compassion.org/Self_Compassion_Scale_for_ researchers.pdf.

2. Scoring/scoring interpretations adapted from Kristin D. Neff, "Test How Self-Compassionate You Are," http://www.self-compassion.org.

About the Author

Darlene Lancer is a licensed marriage and family therapist and author of *Codependency for Dummies* and two e-books: *How to Speak Your Mind: Become Assertive and Set Limits* and *10 Steps to Self-Esteem: The Ultimate Guide to Stop Self-Criticism.* As a relationship and codependency expert, Ms. Lancer has counseled individuals and couples for twenty-five years and coaches internationally. She frequently gives seminars on self-esteem, relationships, and codependency and is sought after nationally to speak to professional groups and radio audiences. Her articles appear in professional journals and Internet mental health websites, including on her own, www.whatiscodependency.com.

About Hazelden Publishing

As part of the Hazelden Betty Ford Foundation, Hazelden Publishing offers both cutting-edge educational resources and inspirational books. Our print and digital works help guide individuals in treatment and recovery, and their loved ones. Professionals who work to prevent and treat addiction also turn to Hazelden Publishing for evidence-based curricula, digital content solutions, and videos for use in schools, treatment programs, correctional programs, and electronic health records systems. We also offer training for implementation of our curricula.

Through published and digital works, Hazelden Publishing extends the reach of healing and hope to individuals, families, and communities affected by addiction and related issues.

For more information about Hazelden publications,
please call **800-328-9000**
or visit us online at **hazelden.org/bookstore**

Other titles that may interest you:

Codependent No More
How to Stop Controlling Others and Start Caring for Yourself
Melody Beattie
The healing touchstone of millions, this modern classic holds the key to understanding codependency and to unlocking its stultifying hold on your life.
Order No. 5014 (softcover)
Also available as an e-book and app.

The Language of Letting Go
Daily Meditations on Codependency
Melody Beattie
Melody Beattie integrates her own life experiences and fundamental recovery reflections in this daily meditation book written especially for those of us who struggle with the issue of codependency.
Order No. 5076 (softcover)
Also available as an e-book and app.

Beyond Codependency
And Getting Better All the Time
Melody Beattie
In simple, straightforward terms, Beattie takes you into the territory beyond codependency, into the realm of recovery and relapse, family-of-origin work and relationships, surrender and spirituality.
Order No. 5064 (softcover)
Also available as an e-book.

Hazelden books are available at fine bookstores everywhere. To order from Hazelden, call **800-328-9000** or visit **hazelden.org/bookstore.**
For more information about our mobile apps, visit hazelden.org/web /public/mobileapps.page.